HOPE
Against Darkness

*The Transforming
Vision of Saint Francis
in an Age of Anxiety*

RICHARD ROHR
with John Feister

Franciscan
MEDIA
Cincinnati, Ohio

Scripture citations are taken from the *Jerusalem Bible*, copyright ©1966 by Darton, Longman & Todd, Ltd., and Doubleday, a division of Random House, Inc., and from the *New Jerusalem Bible*, copyright ©1985 by Darton, Longman & Todd, Ltd., and Doubleday, a division of Random House, Inc. Reprinted by permission.

Much of "Francis of Assisi—Showing the Way Toward Reconstruction" first appeared in *Sojourners* magazine.

"The Great Chain of Being" was originally published in *Radical Grace* (newsletter for the Center for Action and Contemplation in Albuquerque, N.M.), October/November 1997, and the section entitled "What Is Behind Hate?" in Chapter Ten first appeared in *Radical Grace,* March/April 2000.

We are grateful to the following publishers for permission to reprint:

The Tablet, the international Catholic weekly, for excerpts from "Oh, to Be a Victim," by Andrew Greeley,   copyright ©1997 by *The Tablet*

Harcourt Brace Jovanovitch and Faber and Faber for excerpts from "Burnt Norton" by T. S. Eliot, copyright ©1971 by Esme Valerie Eliot

Paulist Press for excerpts from *Bonaventure,* Ewert Cousins, editor and translator, copyright ©1978

Loretta Ross-Gotta for her poem "In Praise of Boundaries"

Franciscan Press for excerpts from *English Omnibus of the Sources for the Life of St. Francis,* edited by Marion A. Habig, copyright ©1973 by Franciscan Herald Press

Cover design by Candle Light Studios
Book design by Constance Wolfer

ISBN: 978-0-86716-485-5

Published by Franicscan Media
28 W. Liberty Street
Cincinnati, OH 45202
www.FranciscanMedia.org

Printed in the United States of America.

DEDICATED TO ARCHBISHOP DESMOND TUTU

man of hope,

inspired by Francis

Other works by Richard Rohr, available from Franciscan Media:

Books

Breathing Under Water: Spirituality and the Twelve Steps
Eager to Love: The Alternative Way of Francis of Assisi
From Wild Man to Wise Man: Reflections on Male Spirituality (with Joseph Martos)
The Great Themes of Scripture: New Testament (with Joseph Martos)
The Great Themes of Scripture: Old Testament (with Joseph Martos)
Jesus' Plan for a New World: The Sermon on the Mount (with John Feister)
Preparing for Christmas: Daily Meditations for Advent
Silent Compassion: Finding God in Contemplation
Why Be Catholic? Understanding Our Experience and Tradition (with Joseph Martos)
Wondrous Encounters: Scripture for Lent
Things Hidden: Scripture as Spirituality
Yes, And…: Daily Meditations

Audiobooks

A Spirituality for the Two Halves of Life (with Paula D'Arcy)
Adam's Return: The Five Promises of Male Initiation
Breathing Under Water: Original Audio Presentation
Breathing Under Water: Spirituality and the Twelve Steps
Eager to Love: The Alternative Way of Francis of Assisi
Fire From Heaven: A Retreat for Men
Great Themes of Paul: Life as Participation
Great Themes of Paul: Life as Participation
Healing Our Violence through the Journey of Centering Prayer (with Thomas Keating, O.C.S.O.)
Jesus and His Church
Letting Go: A Spirituality of Subtraction
Men and Women: The Journey of Spiritual Transformation
New Great Themes of Scripture
On Pilgrimage: Lourdes, Holy Land, Assisi, and Rome
Preparing for Christmas: Daily Meditations for Advent
Rebuild the Church: Richard Rohr's Challenge for the New Millennium
Richard Rohr on Scripture
Richard Rohr on Transformation
Sermon on the Mount
Silent Compassion: Finding God in Contemplation
The Spiritual Family and the Natural Family
The Spirituality of Imperfection
Things Hidden: Scripture as Spirituality
True Self / False Self
Wondrous Encounters: Scripture for Lent

DEUS MEUS ET OMNIA

. . . .

MY GOD–AND *ALL* THINGS

–motto of the Franciscans

Table of Contents

· · · · · · · · · · · · · · · · · · · ·

The authors would like to acknowledge the inspiration and constant encouragement of Jeremy Harrington, O.F.M., and the talented editing of April Bolton.

This book began in the audiocassette series, Rebuild the Church: Richard Rohr's Challenge for the New Millennium *(St. Anthony Messenger Press). Chapter Two was adapted from a talk Richard gave at the Archdiocese of Los Angeles Religious Education Congress in 1998. All of the material was rewritten, added to and somewhat reorganized for this book. The authors apologize for any shortcomings in making the transition from speech to the written word.*

PART ONE

The Current Dilemma

. . . .

ONE REASON so many people have lost heart today is that we feel both confused and powerless. The forces against us are overwhelming: consumerism, racism, militarism, individualism, patriarchy, the corporate juggernaut. These "powers and principalities" seem to be fully in control. We feel helpless to choose our own lives, much less a common life, or to see any overarching meaning in it all.

This became all the more evident after the horrific terrorist attacks of September 11, 2001. Everything that had seemed so important—stock options, consumer choices, increasingly affluent lifestyles—suddenly faded. Church attendance increased immediately. Religious Web sites experienced a surge in activity. We saw a wave of patriotism unseen for decades. Some people even had the courage to look into our collective conscience and start questioning if the developed nations have been doing enough to help eradicate poverty worldwide. All of it points to a long-standing, deep need in our society that we must face with more urgency.

More than anything else, I believe, we are facing a crisis of meaning. The world seems so complex, and we seem so small. What can we do but let the waves of history carry us and try to keep afloat somehow?

But maybe we can at least look to that same history for some patterns, or for those who found the patterns. That is the thesis of this book, and in that sense it is a very traditional book, even though many of these patterns point to revolutionary suggestions. I am going to point particularly to the man who has one of the longest bibliographies of anyone in history: a thirteenth-century Italian called Francis of Assisi. He must have had some kind of genius to have attracted so many cultures and religions, and to be contemporary in so many of his responses eight hundred years later.

Saint Francis of Assisi stepped out into a world being recast by the emerging market economy. He lived amid a decaying old order in which his father was greedily buying up the small farms of debtors, moving quickly into the new entrepreneurial class. Francis stepped into a Church that seems to have been largely out of touch with the masses. But he trusted a deeper voice and a bigger truth. He sought one clear center and moved out from there.

The one clear centerpiece was the Incarnate Jesus. He understood everything else from that personalized reference point. Like Archimedes, Francis had found his one firm spot on which to stand and from which he could move his world. He did this in at least three clear ways.

First, he walked into the prayer-depths of his own tradition, as opposed to mere religious repetition of old formulas. Second, he sought direction in the mirror of creation itself, as opposed to mental and fabricated ideas or ideals. And, most radically, he looked to the underside of his society, to the "community of those who have suffered," for an understanding of how God transforms us. In other words, he found *depth and breadth—and a process to keep you there.*

The depth was an inner life where all shadow, mystery and paradox were confronted, accepted and forgiven. Here he believed God could be met in fullness and truth. The breadth was the actual world itself, a sacramental universe. It was not the ideal, the churchy or the mental, but the right-in-front-of-you-and-everywhere—the *actual* as opposed to the ideal.

And, finally, he showed us the process for staying there—the daring entrance into the world of human powerlessness. His chosen lens was what he called "poverty" and, of course, he was only imitating Jesus. He set out to read reality through the eyes and authority of those who have "suffered and been rejected"—and come out resurrected. This is apparently the "privileged seeing" that allows you to know something that you can know in no other way. It is the unique baptism that Jesus says we must all be baptized with (see Mark 10:39). My assumption in this book is that this is the "baptism" that transforms. It is larger than any religion or denomination. It is taught by the Spirit in reality itself.

One can argue doctrinally about many aspects of Jesus, but you cannot say he was not a poor man, that he did not favor the perspective from the "bottom" as a privileged viewpoint. All other heady arguments about Jesus must deal with this overwhelming given. Francis did. It became his litmus test for all orthodoxy and for ongoing transformation into God. Who would have thought of it, except God?

For Francis, the true "I" had, first of all, to be discovered and realigned (the prayer journey into the True Self). Then he had to experience himself situated inside of a meaning-filled cosmos (a sacramental universe). Finally, he had to be poor (to be able to read reality from the side of powerlessness).

Francis taught us, therefore, that the antidote to confusion and paralysis is always a return to simplicity, to the actual right-in-front-of-you, to the naked obvious. Somehow he had the genius to reveal what was hidden in plain sight. It was so simple that it was hard to get there. And it will take the rest of this book to explain such simplicity!

The Age of 'the Mind'

What we call the modern age emerged in the eighteenth-century Enlightenment. It was the age of rationalism. The Enlightenment produced a wonderful scientific mind. Its materialist worldview taught us how to measure things. Belief hinged on what could be proven by a certain paradigm called science. Science assumed—and this became the arrogance of the modern mind—that it knew more than anybody else ever had! It did not yet realize that this new knowing was in one small area, and in its new-found excitement it quickly neglected several other areas. Analysis of parts became more important than the synthesis of the whole.

We have been dazzled by our new abilities to know for three centuries now. The modern mind is enthralled at its ability to make things happen, to rearrange genes and chromosomes and atoms, and being able to predict outcomes feels like an almost godly power—and it is. It led us to a philosophy of progress, as opposed to most cyclic or paschal worldviews.

In this more Asian (where all the great religions came from) worldview of harmony, death and life, along with everything else, need only be kept in balance. We would prefer to think that we can almost overcome the death mystery. Moderns believed that things would only get better and better. This worldview took many surrogate forms, but in general is what we know as the modern world. It formed all of us deeply, especially in the West. It told us that education, reason and science would make the world a better place.

But then the Holocaust happened in the very country that was perhaps the most educated, logical and reason-loving in the world. For Europeans the collapse into postmodern thinking began at that point: "If we can be this wrong, maybe nothing is right. All our major institutions failed us."

For Americans, by reason of our isolation from the absurdity of war, our immense power and our incorrigible innocence, we remained in the modern era until the late 1960's. I remember teachers in primary school telling me in the 1950's that we would have overcome all major diseases by the turn of the century. But it has not turned out that way, as we all know. Now, in fact, we have a lot of new diseases and many insolvable diseases of the mind and soul.

For the last thirty years we've begun to speak not of *modernism* but of *postmodernism*—a critique of modernism's false optimism and trust in progress. We're in the postmodern period now, at least in Europe and North America and those countries influenced by them (which is, for better or worse, almost everybody). We now see that reading reality simply through the paradigm of science, reason and technological advancement has not served us well. It has not served the soul well; it has not served the heart or the psyche well. It has not served community well. There must be something more than the physical, because mere physics has left us powerful and effective, but also ravaged in the most important areas of our humanity. The inner world of meaning has not been fed.

The soul, the psyche, human relationships seem at this point to be destabilizing almost at an exponential rate. Our society is producing very many unhappy people and unhealthy people. The spread of violence everywhere in society is frightening. We're seeing that the postmodern mind is a deconstructed worldview. It does not know what it is *for,* as much as it knows what it is *against* and what it *fears.* To have a positive vision of life is almost considered naive in most intellectual circles. These folks are not taken seriously. They are considered to be fools.

If we cannot trust in what we thought was logic and reason, if science is not able to create a totally predictable universe, then *maybe there are no patterns*. Suddenly we live in a very scary and even "disenchanted" universe—where no intelligence appears to be in charge, where there is no beginning, middle or end. What's left is merely the private ego with its own attempts at episodic meaning and control. This is the postmodern novel, deconstructivist art and the movies of aimless direction and gratuitous violence. This is the world that most of those formed after the mid-1960's have grown up in. It is starved for meaning, grasping at anything and everything.

To Know and Not to Know

The postmodern mind assumes that nothing is truly knowable, that everything is a social construct or an intellectual construct that will soon be discounted by new information. The irony is that the same postmodernist also believes that he or she knows more than anybody else— that there are no absolutes, no patterns that are always true. You end up with a being who is both godlike ("I know") and utterly cynical ("I have to create my own truth because there are no universal patterns"). This is a terrible dilemma to live under. It is an impossible burden which former peoples never presumed to carry. No wonder depression and suicide now affect even children's lives to such a degree!

Postmodern thinking allows us to discredit and discount everything, which also leaves us in a lonely and absurd state. Philosophically it's called nihilism—*nihil* meaning "nothing." Nihilism affects us all in some way, but most especially those at the top and the bottom of any society. The elite have the freedom to dismiss and discount everything beneath them; the oppressed finally have an explanation for their sad state. We see this tragedy in most of the minority and oppressed groups of the world, and in the addictive entertainment culture of the wealthy. For the rich it's a false high, for the poor a false low, and both are losing.

Stephen Carter, a first-rate cultural critic, accuses many of his own black brothers and sisters and all of America of a nihilistic and inevitably materialistic worldview, except for those who have held onto their religious roots (see *The Culture of Disbelief*, Doubleday Anchor, 1994). We could say this of most Western groups, but only a fellow black could say it of his own. He says there's no belief in anything except power, possessions and prestige in America, while a religious facade is kept up. Michael Lerner, a Jewish philosopher and psychologist, would say much the same to his audience (see *The Politics of Meaning*, Addison-Wesley, 1996).

Another aspect of the postmodern mind is what we call a "market" mentality. In a market-driven culture like ours, things no longer have *inherent value*, but only *exchange value*. "Will it sell? Will it win? Will it defeat the opponent?" These are the first concerns, and sometimes the only concerns, of the *market mind*. It leaves us very empty and shapeless after a few years, while still motivating us for another day. The "Temple" of creation has then become a place of mere buying and selling. No wonder Jesus was driven to rage at such a scene, and consciously made "a whip out of cord" to drive it out (see John 2:15).

Once we lose a sense of inherent value, we have lost all hope of encountering true value, much less the Holy. Even people of religion, if they do not pray, will normally regress to an "exchange value" reading of religion. It is no longer about the Great Mystery, mystic union and transformation, but merely social order and control. Moral codes and priesthoods are enlisted for the sake of enforcement and some measure of civility. For many, if not most, Western Christians, it is basically a "crime and punishment" scenario, instead of the "grace and mercy" world that Jesus proclaims.

This is the only way that the postmodern Christian can put shape into this basically shapeless, bad novel called human life. It looks like an answer, or even gospel, but it is the same old story line of most of history: The big and strong win; Prometheus passes for Jesus. I must admit this was the only gospel I heard in my early seminary training. What a relief to finally study the Gospels and observe the real transformative patterns in humanity!

The final state of a nihilistic worldview is a collapse into vulgarity and shock as the primary values. If there is no criterion of quality, we can at least compensate with quantity (of emotion, violence, sex, sound), which normally devolves into a deep dismissal of almost everything. Soon the concern becomes: "How can I be more outrageous than anyone else?" "How can I laugh at things before they disappoint me?" There are no heroes or heroines, so the individual feels a kind of negative heroism in exposing all human failings, foibles and phoniness. I do not really have to grow up myself, I will find my meaning in pointing out that everyone and everything else is phony. Let's admit this is the character of much of our political life, too. We are all pulling one another downwards in such a scenario, but it is not the downward mobility of humility. It is merely the downward spiral of a universal skepticism. We no longer have the discipline to find the classic forms—nor do we believe there are any.

Strangely this is almost a secular form of Puritanism. We are still trying to expose and hate the sins of the world; they are just defined differently. The sex scandals of Washington are not much different from the old Irish priests preoccupied with ferreting out fornicators in the parish. We think we can dominate over the shadow self rather than forgive it, cover it, transform it, embrace it into a larger wholeness. No wonder that Jesus did not concentrate on the shadow self at all, but almost entirely on the ego!

It is much easier to look for someone to blame, sue, expel or expose when there is no coherent meaning or divine purpose in the world. Someone has to be at fault for my unhappy life! As long as we keep trying to deal with the mystery of evil in some way other than forgiveness and healing, we will continue to create negative ideologies like fundamentalism and nihilism in all their endless forms. One demands perfect order; the other denies that it is even possible. Jesus does neither, but lives on the horns of the human dilemma.

We've all seen things in recent years that not long ago we would have considered unthinkable. And these spectacles are not limited to "gangster rappers" or cultural dropouts by any means. This trend has shown itself in mainstream art and media, in writing and in every aspect of lifestyle: We are no longer expected to submit to the classic disciplines of anything, because there aren't any.

It is one thing to endure the years of discipline that it takes to learn your craft, and then to put paint on paper in new and creative ways. That might, in some cases, rise to great art. *You have to know the rules before you can break the rules.* "Breaking the rules," after all, is often the source of genuine creativity and even genuine holiness. But starting there, throwing paint on the paper as a form of self-expression is not going to stand the test of time. There's nothing there that is tied into collective memory or the archetypal anything. It is just *my* feelings. There is too much of the imperial ego and too little room for anybody else, for anything communal and shareable.

Private feelings are our form of truth today, a kind of ultimate self-absorption—understandable because there are *no universal patterns.* Yet, in expressing private feelings, people really think they've done something great. You see this on the talk shows: You realize those people have never read, studied, prayed or listened to anybody except their own tyrannical feelings. Yet they think they have a right for their *un*informed opinions on the welfare system or religion or nuclear warfare to be taken seriously! No wonder our public discourse is deteriorating, even at the level of the court, the senate, the university and, yes, the Church.

It is true that lots of folks are angry and alienated and have something to say about it, but we've got to listen to some greater minds, some greater hearts, some greater souls who are not just caught in their own self-expression of "this is me," but are also addressing the greater issues of "this is us" and, especially, of the Great Patterns that are always true. (We will discuss these terms more fully in Chapter Five.) Those are the people who will reconstruct. Those are the people worth listening to and talking with—some of whom you will encounter later in this book (see Chapter Thirteen). I think that is what it means to be a part of the great human parade, instead of just an isolated individual, a member of the Cosmic Body of Christ, instead of being designated by that oxymoron, "an individual believer."

If you are an individualist you are surely not a believer, and if you are a believer you are utterly responsible, connected and aligned everywhere. Before we can reconstruct this deconstructed culture, we must be utterly reconnected ourselves. That is the work of healthy religion (*re-ligio* = "re-bind"). Maybe that is another way to describe "submitting to the classic patterns."

Owning Our Cultural Biases

Every viewpoint is a view from a point. Unless we recognize and admit our own personal and cultural viewpoints, we will never know how to decentralize our own perspective, and we will live with a high degree of illusion and blindness, a blindness that brings much suffering into the world. I think this is what Simone Weil meant in saying "the love of God is the source of all truth." Only an outer and positive reference point utterly grounds the mind, or the heart, for that matter.

One of the keys to wisdom is that you must recognize your own biases, your own addictive preoccupations, and those things which, for some reason, you refuse to pay attention to. Until you see these patterns (which is early-stage contemplation), you will never be able *to see what you do not see*. No wonder that Saint Teresa of Avila declared self-knowledge to be the first and necessary entrance way to the "interior castle." Without such critical awareness of the small self, there is little chance that any individual will produce truly great knowing or enduring wisdom.

Postmodernism, in a rage of disappointment, is deconstructing everything in its path to counter the three controlling presuppositions of modernism which formed our age.

(As we will see, deconstruction is having both good and bad effects. We must say up front that there are good meanings to deconstruction! Without some deconstruction, everything becomes idolatrous. The prophets were "religious deconstructionists.")

First, modernism believed that *reality is ordered*. Postmodern thought says there is no order at all. Postmodernism, ironically, is moving closer to both nihilism and mysticism, to the notion that either *no one* is in charge or *someone* else is in charge. All we know is that our logic and reason is clearly not! Thus, the new rise in spiritualities of every style and stripe. The old Churches have lots of competition, whereas they used to have a monopoly.

It strikes me as not accidental that we called priesthood "Holy Orders." The term seems to reveal what we really wanted from priesthood: order, lines of order, boundaries, control, clarity. Not bad qualities of themselves, even much needed qualities, but the desire for them might explain why even the Church was more comfortable with the assumptions of modernism than with this "Holy Disorder" now showing itself. Yet, the cross itself is clearly a proclamation of *disorder* at the heart of reality. True Christianity never believed in either perfect order or total chaos, but a reality fraught with contradictions. It made this mixed world the world of God. Jesus was crucified on "the collision of opposites."

Second, the modern mind believed that *reality is knowable by our human reason*. Nature is predictable and, therefore, to some degree controllable. Quantum physics, however, now says that "indeterminacy," "probability," "chaos theories," Heisenberg's "uncertainty principle" perhaps more truly express the final mystery of reality than classical physics ever did.

This is a great humiliation for the modern mind. Physics has discovered that when you get to the smallest point (atomic particles) and the biggest point (galaxies and black holes)—it's mystery again! It looks knowable, yet finally it's unknowable when you reach the edges. Control eventually gives way to mystery and the letting go of control. Suddenly we are not in charge. Some say that the physicists are becoming mystics, while the clergy are becoming psychologists—both trying to figure out the non-rational responses of most people and the tragic character of most events.

The small scientist stays in the middle and thinks he's living inside an entirely coherent system. The great scientists like Einstein, the "Man of the Century," enter back into mystery. Einstein said, "All I know is, the great truth—when we discover it—*will be simple, and it will be beautiful.*" He never had the arrogance to think he had fully discovered his "unified field theory," the final paradigm that would account for all the forces in the universe. His humble assertion is an act of faith of a great mind, of a great scientist. It reminds one of Dante's image for the heights of paradise: a "white rose." Utter simplicity and utter beauty. It coheres, it holds together. That sense of coherence is what we no longer have.

Great religion always said that the best we could hope for would be metaphor, symbol, image. Here we do not know as much as *we are known*; we do not make the connections as much as realize that *we are connected*. Then we can only kneel and kiss the ground. The logical mind gives up its tyranny.

Deconstructionism, as terrible as it sounds, might well be leading us to the proper humility and simplicity for truly healthy God encounters. Yet, again, the Churches, at least the Roman Church, had grown used to a philosopher's God much more than the biblical God, who scandalizes us with his "particularity," preferences, choices and absolute freedom. Modernism gave us predictability that felt good; now someone else is in charge and we must surrender to both tragedy and utter gratuity. It sounds much more biblical, even if much more scary.

Third, the modern mind believed that *human fulfillment consisted primarily in knowing and discovering all the laws of science and nature*. Modernism said we should utilize them whenever possible, and comply with them when we can't know them or can't change them. In order to move ahead, therefore, all we had to do was increase scientific knowledge. Whether it be medical knowledge or space exploration, we would overcome all difficulty.

Anyone born before 1960 was deeply influenced by that kind of thinking. But we no longer believe it, nor that mere education transforms people. We no longer are so sure that the laws of nature are predictable and that human nature consists in knowing all the laws and controlling the universe as best we can. If you doubt this, simply look at the emergence of superstition and magic, UFO theories, New Age fundamentalism of every sort, shamanic journeys, an actual reveling in the unconscious, the irrational, the non-rational, the symbolic, the "spiritual." And much of this among very educated people! The gods of the body, belly and heart are demanding to be heard, and not just the god of reason.

There's bad news and good news here. Living in a transitional age is scary: It's falling apart; it's unknowable; it doesn't cohere; it doesn't make sense; it's all mystery again; we can't put order in it. This is the postmodern panic. It lies beneath most of our cynicism, our anxiety, our pandemic violence.

Yet, there is little in the biblical revelation that ever promised us an ordered universe. The whole Bible is about meeting God in the *actual*, in the incarnate moment, in the scandal of particularity, and not in educated theories, so much so that it is rather amazing that we ever tried to codify and control the whole thing.

The Bible seems to always be saying that this journey is indeed a journey, a journey always initiated and concluded by God, and a journey of transformation much more than mere education about anything. We would sooner have textbooks, I think. Then the journey would remain a spectator sport, as much religion often seems to be. The education model elicits a low level of commitment and investment, even if it keeps people obedient and orthodox. The transformation model risks people knowing and sharing "the One Spirit that was given us all to drink" (1 Corinthians 12:13). So sad that we have preferred conformity and group loyalty over real change!

But chaos often precedes great creativity. Darkness creates the desire for light. Faith actually precedes great leaps into new knowledge. That's the good news. Our uncertainty is the doorway into mystery, the doorway into surrender, the path to God that Jesus called "faith." (How strange, and actually heresy of the first order, that we turned this dark night of faith into a demand for certitude and control!) I'm seeing people of great faith today, people of the Big Truth, who love the Church, but are no longer on bended knee before an idol. They don't need to worship the institution; neither do they need to throw it out and react against it. This is a great advance in human maturity. Only a few years ago it was always either/or thinking: "If it isn't perfect I'm leaving it." We are slowly discovering what many of us are calling "the Third Way," neither flight nor fight, but the way of compassionate knowing.

Both the way of fight and the way of flight fall short of wisdom, although they look like answers in the heat of the moment. When it's an either/or world you have no ability to transcend, to hold together, to be creative.

The dualistic mind seemingly has a preference for knowing things by comparison. The price we pay for our dualistic mind is that one side of the comparison is always idealized and the other demonized, or at least minimized. There is little room for balance or honesty, much less love. Wisdom, however, is always holding the "rational" and the "romantic" together: Aristotle and Plato, Aquinas and Bonaventure, Freud and Jung, saint and sinner, Spirit and senses.

In fact, you could say that the greater opposites you can hold together, the greater soul you usually have. By temperament, most of us prefer one side to the other. Holding to one side or another frees us from the tension and the anxiety. Only a few dare to hold the irresolvable tension in the middle. It is the "folly" of the cross, where you cannot "prove" you are right, but only "hang" between the good and the bad thieves of every issue, paying the price for their reconciliation (see Luke 23:39 ff.).

The *tertium quid*, the "reconciling third," is very often the Holy Spirit! But as many have said before, the Holy Spirit is the rejected or forgotten member of the Holy Trinity. We don't know how to dogmatize or control wind, water or doves alighting from the sky (see John 3:8). Such deliberate and daring metaphors for God should keep us rightly humble in all our knowing, predicting and explaining.

The *Mysterium Tremendum*

For Christians the abandonment of modernism's certainty is going to be a journey deeper into both biblical religion and the "tremendous mystery" of Jesus. He is the archetype of what it means to be a full human being. He holds together heaven and earth, divine and human, a male body with a female soul. He is a living example of full consciousness, which is precisely to accept the usually rejected unconscious, fear-filled and shadowy parts of reality. He's the son of God and the son of Adam. We need to realize that we also are daughters of God and daughters of earth, of divinity and of flesh, of ego and shadow. Both are good. And they are even better when they are put together. That's why we worship Jesus! He is the icon of what salvation means. When the two can happily coexist within us, one might say that we are "saved."

Our goal ought to be a spirituality connected to this world in every aspect, seeing the Divine Light shining through the mundane, the ordinary, the physical, the material, the entire cosmos—-and not only in the churchy, the correct and the pure, which keeps the world split and contentious. That's the synthesis that I believe healthy Christianity is leading us toward. "When that day comes, the very bells on the horses will be inscribed with the words, 'Sacred to Yahweh,' and the cooking pots of the house of Yahweh will be as holy as the sprinkling bowls before the altar" (Zechariah 14:20).

Paul intuits this when he speaks in Ephesians (4:4-6) of "one Body, one Spirit...one hope...one Lord, one faith, one baptism, and one God who is Father of all, over all, through all and within all." Yet, if I talked that way today, I would be accused in many Catholic circles of pantheism or lightweight humanism. So I just quote Saint Paul.

We have no reason to apologize for our Christ. He is a flawless image, especially in his crucified and risen form, of all that God is doing on earth. He is our living icon of transformation. Jesus holds together the tension of opposites, and in their ultimate shapes of life and death. *Humanity itself could be defined as that which is eternally crucified and eternally resurrected—all at once!*

The cross, as we will see again and again, is the "coincidence of opposites": One movement going vertical, another going horizontal, clearly at cross-purposes. When the opposing energies of any type collide within you, you suffer. If you agree to hold them creatively until they transform you, it becomes redemptive suffering. This stands in clear and total opposition to the myth of redemptive violence, which has controlled most of human history, even though it has never redeemed anything. Expelling the contradictions instead of "forgiving" them only perpetuates the problem. This is so obvious and self-evident that most people cannot see it. Maybe that is why John's Gospel seems to make blindness the primary metaphor for sin.

We're living in a time when the far right and the far left in almost every institution are using the eccentricities and evils of the other end to justify their own extremes. There seems to be an emergence of reactionary and protectionist thinking all over the world, which then serves as justification for people's overreacting on the political left. This ping-pong game has been so common in this century, even within Christianity—which should know better by now—that Christianity, for many, has come to mean anti-intellectual, fanatically narrow-minded people. Christianity, for some, is neither faith nor reason—just reactive tribalism hiding behind the skirts of "Mother Church." How sad if the Great Tradition ever settled for so little.

I move in some circles where the word *Christian*, unfortunately, is a negative adjective. To them "He's a Christian" means he knows nothing about history, nothing about politics, and is probably incapable of civil conversation about anything. Five Bible quotes are the available answers to everything. How did we ever get to this low point after such a tradition of wisdom? How did we ever regress to such arrogance after the humble folly of the cross?

When there is no ability to build bridges to the other, to even understand otherness, we know we are outside the pale of authentic Christianity. Surely Jesus came for more than self-congratulative societies who forever circle the wagons around their own saved identity and their own self-serving god!

Such trivializations of God's greatness deserve to be ignored and avoided, even when the Churches themselves get involved in such partisanship. Don't waste time fighting it directly or you will become its casualty. Our motto is simple and clear: *The best criticism of the bad is the practice of the better.* Just go ahead and live positively "in God, through God, with God." In time the fruits will be apparent. In the short run, you will hold the unresolved tension of the cross. In the long run, you will usher in something entirely new and healing. This was the almost intuitive spiritual genius of Saint Francis. He wasted no time attacking the rich Churches and pretentious clergymen, or even greedy tradesmen like his dad; he just went to the side and did it differently. He is remembered forever; they are lost to history.

A Lonesome World

I'll conclude this chapter with a look at a sad by-product of postmodernism: loneliness. Postmodernism and modernism reject a personalized universe. They *dis-enchant* the universe. You no longer expect miracles; you no longer expect the transcendent to shine through the tree and the leaf, with "every common bush afire with God." This is our modern state of alienation and anxiety and what the French call *ressentiment. Ressentiment* describes a world that is no longer safe, no longer sacred and no longer home. It is disconnected, fragile and, therefore, always ready to take offense. The experience of the alienated member of society is "I'm alone" and "I have to figure it all out." The secular world is no longer abundant enough or safe enough to imagine a win/win scenario. Everything is zero sum—all winding down. Our world's only story line is win/lose, but unfortunately it actually ends up to be lose/lose.

Yet, this very secular and empty worldview longs for the opposite. Have you noticed how often the newsmagazines covered religious stories, angels, saints, miracles during the past few years? American Greetings, one of the largest greeting-card companies, recently added a line of spiritual and religious cards, noting a "new trend" in America. We know this world is too dead, too empty, too disenchanted—it's not enough for us, we're not at home without our spiritual nature.

Some understanding of this often comes together for people very clearly at the end of their lives. Not long ago I was with my mother when she passed away. At one point before her death she was seeing angels. Now my mother is no sentimentalist. She's an *eight* on the Enneagram, a Kansas earth woman and an utter realist. I probably got my no-nonsense Catholicism from her. But about a week before she died, she started seeing angels, even my guardian angel. (When you get close to the end, they say the veil gets very thin between the worlds.)

My mother, at the end, would use the word *home* so much. She'd tell my father to come over to her sickbed and say, "Take me home." He thought she meant to drive her across town to her house, since she spent her final days at my brother's house. Then we understood after a while that home meant something different.

The sadness of modern people is that they don't feel at home. No wonder we have Doctor Kevorkians. Euthanasia, abortion, capital punishment and war itself will only increase unless there's a larger story like the paschal mystery that gives transcendent meaning to human suffering. The soul must expand, it seems, so that we can carry the great mystery of God. "We must learn to bear the beams of love," as William Blake would say. That learning is usually, I am sorry to say, in the realm of suffering. It seems to be the only thing strong enough to make us surrender control and what we call logic.

God makes grace out of our grit, salvation out of our sin. We are saved, ironically, not by doing it right as much as by the suffering of having done it wrong. We come to God not through our perfection (thank God!) as much as through our imperfection. Finally, all must be forgiven and reconciled. Life does not have to be fixed, controlled or even understood for me to be happy. Now, be honest, that *is* good news! In fact, what else would be?

The gospel is a new "logic" that "The Fool on the Hill," as in Lennon and McCartney's song, brought to the world. This gospel logic is much broader, much deeper, much more spacious and filled with more compassion than any system of thought that the world has been able to create. Maybe that is what truth means. Why would anyone settle for the small mind of rationalism or the no-mind of non-rationalism? This is the Great Mind of Christ.

CHAPTER TWO

Beyond Victimhood

. . . .

MANY PEOPLE in many parts of our world are clearly carrying the cross today. For those in poverty perhaps it is the cross of deep social injustice. For us in the affluent countries it's more likely that we carry the crosses of broken relationships and broken psyches. But the thing I find in common is that for most people it doesn't feel like the cross. It just feels like pain.

I know that every age has had its pain, but spirituality in its best sense is about *what you do with your pain*. We do not know what to do with it any more. The "machine" that transformed our pain into something better seems to have disappeared. In a culture with no Transcendent Center, there is no one to hand pain over to. In a culture with no cross/resurrection image, there is no meaning to our suffering. When a people no longer knows that God *is*, God is *good*, God can be *trusted* and God is *on your side*, we frankly have very serious problems. Our pain is going to go shooting in all directions, none of them good. That's where we are today.

I remember a woman once came to me who, by her own admission, was becoming a rather hateful and negative person, both in her family and in her job. And as long as we talked she kept coming back to this seemingly irresolvable pain, this injustice that she had experienced, rightly or wrongly, truthfully or untruthfully. But one moment an admission slipped out of her mouth: "My pain is my ticket." As we talked it through I realized, and I think she did too, that her pain had become her very identity. She seemed to know that to play the victim gave her a kind of power, an instant moral superiority over almost everybody. Strangely, she had become untouchable and invulnerable.

Although individuals have probably often done this, it is only in the last fifty years that it has become a cultural fad. Now we even have "inherited victimhood." You gain all kinds of immediate credit because somebody's great-grandmother did something to your great-grandmother's generation.

This is probably the ultimate form of moral blackmail. All you have to do, in this strange configuration of life, is prove that you are a victim and you immediately have the moral high ground. You can also cop out and do nothing, because you now carry this paralyzing wound. In either case, you stop growing and make life miserable for all around you.

Playing the victim is an effective way of getting moral high ground without doing any moral development whatsoever. You don't have to grow up, you don't have to let go, you don't have to forgive, you don't have to surrender—-all the things that great religion deemed necessary. Now you just have to accuse somebody else of being worse than you are, or of being a member of a race or group that is worse than yours, and that makes you feel like you're good, moral or superior. To prove that someone else is a sinner gives some people the strange experience—obviously not true—that they are above all that sort of thing.

Let me give several examples that I've read in the British Catholic magazine *The Tablet*. In an essay by Andrew Greeley, "Oh, to be a Victim" (March 1997), the subject was this victim phenomenon. (Don't be offended too quickly: If you could read all the way through, you would see that the article doesn't try to take one side or the other of any contemporary issue. Rather, it shows we can all play the victim on either side of any issue to seek moral high ground.)

Victimhood to Greeley is a twist on the old sin of pride. "'I am from the Third World. You are from the First World. You have exploited us for centuries. Therefore you are guilty of exploitation, indeed of exploiting me. Therefore I am morally superior to you and I have power in our relationship.'" This is a form of power, but it's not the power that Jesus is offering us from the cross.

Second, "'I am a woman. You are a man. Men have oppressed women always. Therefore you [as an individual man] are an oppressor. In fact you are oppressing me. Confess your guilt, not that it will do you any good.'" That's a little unfair, but he wants to give you the feeling, I guess.

"'I am an African American. You are a white American. Your ancestors brought mine here as slaves. You are responsible for the sufferings of African Americans and for my suffering. Do not try to defend yourself. As a white person you are by definition a racist.'…'I am Jewish. You are German. Your ancestors killed my people. You must acknowledge your guilt for what they did and your moral inferiority to me. You claim that your ancestors died in a German concentration camp? That will do you no good. The German nation was and is responsible for the Holocaust. You are presumed to be anti-Semitic and don't try to prove yourself innocent because you can't.'

"'I am a Native American. You are a white American. Your people committed genocide against my people. You must confess your own personal responsibility for that sin and concede me my moral superiority.' ...'I am gay. You are straight. Therefore I am morally superior to you.' 'I am a Palestinian Arab. You are Jewish. Therefore I am morally superior to you.'"

And on and on and on. Victims have found a way to be superior. The rest of us must concede them moral power—at least if they are fashionable victims. Fashion, as we all know, changes every few years.

Although it has become a uniquely American form of entitlement, it does not work in much of the rest of the world. I suspect it would only emerge where the gospel has at least been heard (introducing empathy for the victim) and can now be turned around to personal advantage. It probably only works where people are also rather rich and individualistic, jockeying for power in superficial ways. But it's clearly a major distortion of this symbol that hangs in churches and homes across the land.

The cross became our company logo more than something that we *gazed upon* and *were transformed by. Jesus neither played the victim nor created victims. He became a saving and forgiving victim.*

Inherited and entitled victimhood will get us nowhere. It simply keeps us playing the old game of power in a new, very subtle and disturbing way. It is not the way of powerlessness that Jesus taught us from the cross. It is pretending to be powerless, but, in fact, for the sake of power and control over others. It is the disguise and deterioration of the beautiful, and always scary, message of Jesus. Half of the message is often more problematic than total ignorance. Half of the message safely inoculates you from the whole. Total ignorance often leaves you wide open for conversion. Thus, we have Jesus' shocking statements about prostitutes and sinners (Matthew 21:31), who knew they were "out of it." We call this "beginner's mind," and it is always a head-start, spiritually speaking.

The pattern in most of previous history, and even unfortunately afterwards, was somewhat different. Most human pain has been transmitted to others, I think it is fair to say. It is normally easier to expel our anxiety, our shame, by projecting it onto somebody else. "Let them carry it. I don't want to," we say unconsciously. And it sort of works! We feel relieved by having an enemy or a problem out there. It gives us focus and identity.

René Gírard says that this scapegoating mechanism can be seen as the central story line of human history, a subject to which we will return. In fact, the schedule of wars and "who killed who" is what most people have called history! We never cared much about herstory, the story of those who built the pyramids, the stories from the side of the losers. (That, by the way, is what is so unique about much of the Bible.)

One of the few generalizations we can make in the field of universal spirituality is this: *No one else is your problem*. You are always the locus of conversion and transformation. It is always about *you* first of all. Always. You can even use that as a good litmus test for authentic spirituality. Is it keeping you listening for God? Is it keeping your own feet to the fire? Then it is probably healthy teaching. Is it leading you to suspicion, paranoia, accusation and blaming? Then it is from the "Accuser," which is a quite significant New Testament name for Satan (Revelation 12:10). The Evil One is not only an Accuser, therefore, but also a "father of lies" (John 8:44). Because the other one is not your problem, even though Evil would prefer to have you think so. It keeps you from your own needed transformation and keeps the contentious spirit alive.

Jesus did the victim thing right. He neither played the victim for his own self-aggrandizement nor did he make victims of other people. He became the liberating and forgiving victim. This pattern is quite rare, but whenever it happens, it exercises an immense healing and reconciling influence, even though it often increases the wrath and denial of some accusers. Just read the lives of Martin Luther King, Oscar Romero or Gandhi for the most visible examples from our recent past. Normally, the prophets are killed because they bring the lie out into the open. At that point our hatred is pointed toward the messenger, because he or she has taken away our needed object of hatred. If you need to hate, you will destroy anyone who tells you your hatred is the problem.

The message of the crucified Jesus is a statement about *what to do with your pain now*. What we've done for some strange reason is make Jesus into the one who could keep us from pain *later*. We've missed the entire transformative message! Now it is only a message of gambling and bargaining with God, and attending religious services, often for people with low-level resentment who clearly do not want to be there (ask any parish priest!). Somehow Jesus becomes the great problem-solver and answer-giver for the next world and not primarily the one who teaches us how to live with peace and freedom in this world. It's fire-insurance religion instead of a banquet-right-now. That is a big, big difference, an entirely different agenda.

In the final book of the Bible, the Book of Revelation, we have this recurring image of the Lamb of God (for example, 5:6). He stands on the altar in the center of a cosmic liturgy. Christians are familiar with this symbol: the lamb who is *simultaneously* slaughtered and standing. That paradox is the message of the gospel, the message of the cross: We are simultaneously—in one and the same moment—slaughtered and victorious. You could hardly find an older church which did not have this image somewhere in the liturgical space, and yet one wonders how many people ever understood its archetypal meaning, and why it was the key to opening the "seven seals" usually draped underneath. The Lamb image reveals *the lie of ignorant killing* that has characterized most of human history. And even more, it gives us a way out.

Zealots and Pharisees

To sum up, there seem to be two common avoidances of conversion or transformation, two typical diversionary tactics that we humans use to avoid holding the pain: fight or flight.

The way of *fight* is what I'll call the way of Simon the zealot, and often the way of the cultural liberal. These folks want to change, fix, control and reform other people and other events. The zealot is always looking for the evil, the political sinner, the unjust one, the oppressor, the bad person over there. The zealot permits himself or herself righteously to attack them, to hate them, even to kill them. And when they do, they will think they are "doing a holy duty for God" (John 16:2).

You can take it as a general rule that *when you don't transform your pain you will always transmit it.* Zealots and contemporary liberals often have the right conclusion, but their tactics and motives are often filled with self, power, control and the same righteousness that they hate in conservatives. Basically, they want to *do something* to avoid holding the pain until it transforms them. Because of this too common pattern, I have come to mistrust almost all righteous indignation and moral outrage. In my experience, it is hardly ever from God.

"Resurrected" people prayerfully bear witness against injustice and evil—but also agree compassionately to hold their own complicity in that same evil. It is not over there, it is here. It is our problem, not *theirs*. The Risen Christ, not accidentally, still carries the wounds in his hands and side.

We've all been there at different times—I know I've been there: trying to drive out "the devil" with your own "prince of devils." You're actually energized by having an enemy, someone to hate, because it takes away the inner shame, relieves your inner anxiety.

It gives you, strangely enough, a very false sense of control and superiority, because you've spotted the evil and, thank God, it's over there. As long as *they* are the problem and you can keep your focus on changing them, correcting them, expelling them as the contaminating element, then you can sit in a reasonably comfortable position. But it's a position that the saints called *pax perniciosa*, a dangerous and false peace. It feels like peace, but it's not a true peace. It is the peace of avoidance, denial and projection. The peace of the Crucified comes from holding the tension; the dangerous peace comes from expelling it elsewhere or denying the pain. Yet, to the untrained it feels like peace.

It has taken us a long time to realize that we cannot afford to hate because we become a mirror-but-disguised-image of the same. Once you let the other determine the energy and agenda, you can only react to it, and soon you are the same energy and the same agenda. But *you* can't see it.

Which leads us to the second diversionary tactic: the way of *flight*. This is the common path of the "pharisee," the uninformed, the falsely innocent and often the conservative type. They deny the pain altogether, they refuse to carry the shadow side of anything in themselves or in their chosen groups. There will be no uncertainty, there will be no ambiguity. There will be no problems. It is a form of narcotic, and sometimes probably necessary to get through the day.

But the flight people are also subject to hypocrisy, projection or just plain illusion: "We are right and you are wrong... The world is divided into black and white and I know who the good guys and bad guys are... It's all figured out in my head, and fortified with well-fed emotions and like-minded people." These attitudes can generate huge energy, identity and perseverance. One sits on a pedestal of purity and false innocence. Who would want to leave, if not for a major humiliation that possibly forces you into the pain? Paul symbolically had to be thrown to the ground and have scales fall from his eyes to admit that he was a self-serving Pharisee.

Denial is an understandable way of coping and surviving. It is often the only way that many people can deal with the complexity of their human situation. Sometimes when you conscientize (to arouse political consciousness) the poor or do social analysis for the happily naive middle class, you wonder if you are not just creating psychic problems for them. Wouldn't it be better if they did not know? Now they will only be angry and dissatisfied. That is the dangerous path of enlightenment.

The question is now more daring yet. How can I know, work through the anger and still be a life-giving presence? Naiveté is different from second naiveté. The first is a kind of virtuous ignorance; the latter is a spirit of informed openness, often gained after disillusionment. In fact, between the two there is all the difference in the world. But, normally, we are so sure that people will not be able to work through to true enlightenment that we avoid telling them the whole truth. Or they avoid knowing the whole truth. It is much, much easier *not* to know. Jesus himself understood from the cross: "Father, forgive them, they do not know" (Luke 23:34). They really don't know! But Jesus took the harder path, to know and still forgive, and still understand.

That is the *Third Way*, beyond fight and beyond flight, and yet in a certain sense including both of them. It's fighting in a new way from within, and fleeing from the quick, egocentric response. Only God can hold such an act together within us. The small self is always too small. Only the True Self, which we will return to later in this book, can live the gospel.

Maybe our greatest disservice has been that we have given the Law and the gospel to the fragile self that is incapable even of understanding it. We ended up condemning people to subterfuge, denial, mental gymnastics and trivialization—*by preaching the Law without also offering people that "identity transplant" that we call the gospel!* The Third Way is impossible except for the True Self, "hidden with Christ in God" (Colossians 3:3). Paul took most of his Letter to the Romans to struggle with this dilemma. Law without gospel actually paralyzes and condemns to failure.

What Do We Do With Our Fear?

Our age has been called the age of anxiety, and I think it's probably a good description for this time. We no longer know where our foundations are. When we're not sure what is certain, when the world and our worldview keep being redefined every few months, we're going to be anxious. We want to get rid of that anxiety as quickly as we can. Yet, to be a good leader of anything today—to be a good pastor, a good bishop or, I'm sure, a good father or mother—you have to be able to contain, to hold patiently a certain degree of anxiety. Probably the higher the level of leader you are, the more anxiety you must be capable of holding. Leaders who cannot hold anxiety will never lead you to anyplace new.

That's probably why the Bible says so often, "Do not be afraid." I have a printout that actually proves the phrase appears 365 times! If you cannot calmly hold a certain degree of anxiety you will always be looking for somewhere to expel it. Expelling what you can't embrace gives you an identity, but it's a negative identity. It's not life energy, it's death energy. Formulating what you are against gives you a very quick, clear and clean sense of yourself. Thus, most people fall for it. People more easily define themselves by what they are against, by who they hate, by who else is wrong, instead of by what they believe in and by whom they love.

I hope you see from this common pattern how different the alternative is. You might catch anew the radical and scary nature of faith, because faith only builds on that totally positive place within, however small. It needs an interior "Yes" to begin, just as the "Yes" of Mary began the entire process of salvation. God needs just a mustard seed place that is *in love*, that is open to grace, that is thrilled, that has found something wonderful. You've got to go back and build from that "Yes" place—or faith is not faith. And that's why faith is always rare. Religious group-identity becomes its most common replacement. Then we don't have to find and live from a positive and loving place. We can just go to church.

It's much easier to build our identity on our group, our wounds, our angers, our agenda, our fear; that's the more normal way, unless you've been taught the way of Jesus. Almost everybody takes the easier way, because in the short run it works better. The activist might look powerful and sometimes even have a passion for social justice. But when you draw close, sometimes you find out this isn't a person in love with God, but a person who is basically angry, oppositional or invested in their own agenda. Maybe it's a necessary anger, but that's not yet the freedom of the gospel. Political correctness does not approach the immense gift and power of the gospel, yet educated people often confuse them. Education is not the same as transformation.

This is not to dismiss or make light of real issues of injustice. Are we not to act until we are sure that our motivation is one hundred percent pure? Should we dismiss mere humanists? Of course not! God uses all of us with our mixed motives—me, too. It is just that we have been given, not just the conclusion, but the way to get there also. We have been shown how to fight hate without becoming hate ourselves. We have been given a Companion and a Friend and not just a good idea. We have been given joy in the midst of failure, and not just a way of winning or being right. Gospel people are basically indestructible.

Some time ago I was in Northern Ireland where I had a whole series of retreats and conferences. How deeply many of the Irish people now seem to understand this Third Way. In Northern Ireland they've lived this ping-pong game for generations, sawing the log in the same place back and forth, with nothing new happening. The old is forever repeated. Each killing becomes a justification for another killing, and another slaughter. But now my violence is okay because your violence was wrong.

Don't we see that there's got to be a way out of this stupidity? When both are blind, we both fall into the pit. Vengeance seems so logical, but it doesn't really work: It doesn't advance human history. The wonder of the resurrection stories in the Gospels is that Jesus has no punitive attitude toward the authorities or his cowardly followers, and that the followers themselves never call for any kind of holy war against those who killed their leader. Something new has clearly transpired in history. This is not the common and expected story line. All Jesus does is breathe forgiveness.

It's interesting that Jesus identifies forgiveness with breathing, the one thing that you have done constantly since you were born and will do until you die. He says God's forgiveness is like breathing. Forgiveness is not apparently something God does, it is who God *is*. God can do no other.

An Age of Dubious Information

When I was a little Catholic boy, I thought that forgiveness was for the sake of obtaining some kind of possible or supposed moral purity and re-achieved worthiness. Now I believe that forgiveness in the teaching of Jesus is not for the sake of moral purity; it's quite simply for the sake of a future. There is no hope in most countries I visit. It's almost as if there is no future for this planet. Without the mystery of forgiveness and healing, we are on a straight and now rather quick road toward mutual and justified destruction.

In fact, in the last twenty or thirty years, we've had better scholarship, more honest history and more access to historical records. We now can cite chapter and verse of how and when other people have oppressed us and done us wrong. We have better knowledge than ever before of why we have a right to our anger and wounds. This type of progress will not create any kind of future.

I am surely happy for the honest scholarship and the access, but it is actually a two-edged sword, like all things, cutting good and cutting bad. Only people of wisdom know how to take the helpful information so we can stop victimizing in the future and not be trapped inside the resentful information allowing us to justify new victimizations.

René Gírard says that in the twentieth century we have moved scapegoating to ever-higher levels of disguise and sophistication. Without inner transformation, this is almost inevitable. Education of itself does not assure we will not scapegoat. Many Ph.D.'s were still able to hate men, the rich, blacks and Jews in this century.

Is it possible that we're tearing ourselves apart in this country in our politics, in our Church because there's no one out there to hate right now? We know that even personally we focus much better during a time of crisis. We like a clear enemy, and when the enemy is not clear, it is everywhere. Note the rise in home militias in America after the fall of the Berlin Wall.

Yet, in the supposed peace of today, fear is everywhere. The search for the appropriate enemy is rather non-stop and frantic. It seems the enemy is everywhere because the fear is unnamed and looking for a place to roost. Heads of state, once rather immune, are now the targets of choice. The litigious character of American society seems ridiculous to most of the rest of the world. Just pick up tomorrow morning's paper and see how many of the front page articles are not about one person or one group accusing someone else of being morally inferior, wrong or some kind of "sinner." It hasn't changed since Adam scapegoated Eve and Cain killed Abel.

Anthropologically, I am told that religion begins with a distinction: the dividing of the world into the pure and the impure. On that lie, the whole structure builds. Jesus consistently undoes historic religion by touching and consorting and doing the "impure" things. Not much of a founder for a self-respecting religion!

If there isn't a real obvious and clear enemy like we had during the Second World War, we normally focus on something close to home. That's why the worst and most brutal wars tend to be civil wars. That's why most murders are within the family. The deepest hatreds are often toward those inside your own group. We don't know what to do with our paranoia and hatred now that there are no Communists. So now we have school violence and conspiracy theories of every sort. Look at the near hatred between liberals and conservatives in our own Church! The anger that used to safely go toward Nazis and Communists now goes toward homosexuals and abortionists in our own hometowns.

We not only remain fear-filled and hateful when we keep projecting our anxiety elsewhere, we also misdiagnose the real evil, the real problem. We normally substitute it with a smaller, closer problem that we can literally get our hands around.

Someone recently asked me why there seemed to be so many control freaks in the Church. I don't think this phenomenon appears only in the Church; it's everywhere. When we know we're not really trans-forming culture, we're not really changing the world, we're not really having a great deal of influence at the bigger levels, we move to the level of micro-management. We find some little tiny world where we can be in control and right, where we can be pure and clean. We might as well be saying, "I can't clean up the world, so I'm going to at least clean up my living room," or "I cannot really change and influence peo-ple, so I am going to demand total conformity from the pulpit."

Many of us act out some version of this. I empty all my wastebas-kets. It's stupid, it doesn't make a bit of sense, but at least I feel like I am doing something. I can't change the Church, but I can empty my wastebaskets and something's right inside my office. *Faith, however, allows us to hold the tension until we can recognize the true evil—of which we are a part.* That's foundational to all compassionate and non-violent thinking.

To attack the person out there is usually to simply continue the prob-lem, because he or she is a victim, too. The reason people do evil, why they hate, sin, make mistakes is because somewhere they have been hurt, rejected, excluded or wounded. They just keep passing it on. And the cycle repeats and spreads. Jesus, you could say, came to break and even stop the cycle. Punitive behavior only continues the same old game and, I am afraid, most of the Church itself has yet to understand this. We still think it is about forcing conformity instead of seeking true interior transformation. True transformation always demands that *we* pay the price for the other's growth. We would rather punish and coerce a response. God is much more patient.

Original Shame

What we call Original Sin in Genesis perhaps could, in a sense, better be called Original Shame, because the way that Adam and Eve describe themselves is that they feel naked. Then some of the first words of God to his newly created people are, "Who told you that you were naked?" (Genesis 3:11). Next, in a lovely maternal image, God as seamstress sews leather garments for them (3:21). The first thing God does after creation itself is cover the shame of his new creatures. This must name something that is fundamental within us.

We live not just in an age of anxiety, but also in a time of primal shame. I find very few people who do not feel inadequate, stupid, dirty, unworthy. Always when people come to me for counseling or confes-sion they express in one way or another, "If people only knew the things I think, the things I've done, the things I've said, the things I want to do, who would love me?" We all have that terrible feeling of a fundamental unworthiness. I'm sure it takes many different forms, but somehow it seems to take shape in each of our lives.

Guilt, I am told, is about things we have done or not done, but our shame is about the primal emptiness of our very being. Not what we have done, but who we are and who we are not. Guilt is a moral question. Shame, foundational shame at least, is an ontological question. It is not resolved by changing behavior as much as by changing our very self-image, our alignment in the universe. Shame is not about what we do, but where we abide.

Nine out of ten people start with this premise: "If I behave correctly I will one day see God clearly." Yet the biblical tradition is saying the exact opposite: If you see God clearly, you will behave in a good and human way. Your right behavior does not cumulatively lead to your true being; your true being leads to eventual right behavior. We almost all think that good morality will lead to mystical union, but, in fact, mystical union produces correct morality—along with a lot of joy left over. And the greatest surprise is that, sometimes, a bad moral response is the very collapsing of the ego that leads to our falling into the hands of the living God (see Hebrews 10:31).

An Unlikely God

Christians indeed have a strange image of God: a naked, bleeding man dying on a cross. Now let's be honest. If you were going to create a religion, would any of you ever have thought up this image of God? I mean, if I had been setting out to manufacture a religion, I would have manufactured "seven habits for highly effective people." I would have a big sun or a big golden orb for the symbol of God and I would have called God "the Force." But never in a thousand years would I have thought of an image of God as a naked, bleeding, poor man, rejected by society and religion.

We Catholics have grown up and seen the crucifix so many times that we don't realize how off-center it is. It's not what you would think the image of God could be or should be. In fact I don't know if we even like it. I don't know if *I* do. It is not the way I would have preferred to have thought about the world. Is God eccentric here, or is it we who have not diagnosed the human situation correctly?

What question is God trying to answer by giving us a crucified man for a God? What human problem is God trying to reveal and save us from on the cross? We've always said that he was trying to save us from our sin. And of course that's exactly right. As Saint Paul says, Jesus "became sin" to free us from our sin (Romans 8:3 ff.). What then is our "sin"?

I think it might be called "ignorant killing." He reveals both the ignorance and the killing, which are both hidden from us.

Jesus receives our hatred and does not return it. He suffers and does not make the other suffer. He does not first look at changing others, but pays the price of change within himself. He absorbs the mystery of human sin rather than passing it on. He does not use his suffering and death as power *over* others to punish them, but as power *for* others to transform them.

The risen Jesus is the victory fully personified. As the forgiving victim of history, he is himself transformed/resurrected and transforms/resurrects the other. He includes and forgives the sinner instead of hating him and thereby continuing the pattern of hate. He gives us a history and a future beyond the predictable violent. He stops the dance toward inevitable death. "He destroys death forever," as we say at Easter time. He destroys the death that is eating us all alive, that is eating up our hearts. Death is this endless attempt to justify why I have a right to my hurt and why I have a right to my hatred. Yet, he doesn't really cancel death out; he makes a trophy of it. It's as if he takes death and says, "Do you think you are going to use this against Me? To destroy Me? I'm going to use it to love you." It seems God only allows death and evil insofar as God can also use it in our favor. In the Divine Economy nothing is wasted, not even sin, evil or death. This is God's ultimate victory.

In one sense or another, all ancient religions felt we had to spill our blood to get to God. God was distant, demanding and dangerous. God couldn't possibly love me in my radical unworthiness. What we have in the mystery of the crucified Jesus is the turning around of all primal religion. No more human sacrifice, no more animal sacrifice, no more Jansenism (beating yourself so you can be worthy of this God who basically doesn't like you). *Instead of our spilling blood to get to God we have God spilling blood to get to us!* Pray on that for a week. It's enough to transform you.

God is always the initiator. God is always "the hound of heaven" going out after us because God knows our primordial shame. God is always sewing garments to cover up our immense and intense sense of unworthiness. Our very movements toward God are only because God has first moved toward us. In a very true sense, Jesus undid religion forever. He did not found a religion, as much as he regrounded religion in the very sin and stuff of life.

Message of the Cross

I was teaching in the Philippines a few years ago when some of this began to come together for me. I was seeing how many of the poor people there in the barrios still understood this cross as a message of self-punishment. Their interpretation of Christianity sometimes has a feeling of masochism to it, as if self-punishment somehow pleases God. They don't want it to be true, but they fall back into that pre-gospel thinking that we've got to spill blood to earn God's love.

Here is what I wrote in my journal while I was working on an outer island:

> The message of the cross wrongly appears to most people to be passivity, heroic suffering, the cult of martyrdom, doormat theology or refusing to fight, somehow giving up or giving in, but for God. This is very hard to change or renew in peoples' minds. Maybe that's why I find most people really don't believe in the message of the cross as anything practical, desirable or even attractive. It's just something Jesus did once to resolve some heavenly metaphysical transaction that was needed, but it wasn't really an agenda for us or for now. It's something Jesus did to prove God's love for us, and we should therefore admire Jesus. That imagery is powerful and I wouldn't want to take it away. But it's not the whole picture. The cross is about how to fight and not become a casualty yourself. The cross is about being the victory instead of just winning the victory over somebody else.

The gospel is not about winners over losers; the gospel really is about win/win. But very few get the message! I have to admit ashamedly that some people in the business and education world are better at this than some people in the Church. They are beginning to understand that life cannot simply continue to be posited in terms of winners and losers. There has to be a way that we both can advance together. Mothers tend to have a head start in understanding this as a result of negotiating and compromising with their own children—whom they want to love equally and fully.

The cross is a way of winning that tries to bring along your opponent with you. The cross is refusing to hate or to humiliate the other, because that would be only to continue the same pattern and reciprocate the violence. The cross is about authentic newness. It utterly reframes the human question and forces us to redefine what is success. What is it we really want? What is it we're really after?

The cross is about flight, though, in the sense that we refuse the usual and predictable return punch. We flee from the predicted response so that something new and something transformative can perhaps happen. We run from business as usual to reset the agenda, to reframe the question in a more positive way. It is also about fight, but with a whole new definition of what real power is and what real change is.

Traditionally, women have tended to understand this easier than men. Men themselves have been victims in history by being put into military and business worlds where everything was framed in terms of win or lose. It keeps them in the dualistic mindset much longer. The competitive paradigm became the only way that many men knew how to read reality. They thought that to be a hero meant to win. What the cross was supposed to do for Christians was redefine the true hero and heroine forever. In the first two thousand years, only a small minority of clerics or laity ever got the point. Most of us continued in the old punitive system and, in fact, continued the same story line. By that time, it was in our hard wiring.

The cross is how to work for the answer without becoming part of the problem itself. Look to any number of wars to see why this is right. Even in the struggles of third-world revolutions you see again and again that people search for some kind of economic reform by way of fighting and the use of power. Invariably, when the revolutionaries get into the position of power, they do the same thing that had been done before. Most revolutions begin on the left of the political spectrum and end on the right. This movement is inevitable if the self is not transformed. If the self is not transformed, then it was not really the journey into powerlessness, the mystery of the cross, that inspired their revolution. It was simply another form of dominative power. Jesus is, in some ways, the only true revolutionary. Most revolutions merely rearrange the furniture on the deck of the *Titanic*. Jesus built a new boat.

Unless spirituality answers the questions of power and powerlessness there is never any real reform. There is never any real advancement in human history, because the so-called reformers are done in by the struggle. *The cross is finally about how to stand against hate without becoming hate yourself.*

How can you stand against hate without letting it frame the question? Isn't that the fundamental question for all of us? How do we oppose the evil, the hurts, the betrayals, the abandonment, the rejections, the disappointments in our lives, the people who let us down, the people who turn against us, the people who tell lies about us? How do we stand against that in a way that we do not become a mirror image of the same thing?

The human capacity to hate and kill is *the sin* of the world (John 1:29), and it took a Lamb to dismantle what the lions of history could only perpetuate.

Saint Bonaventure's Coincidence of Opposites

The cross is an image that you can hold on to and draw life from. It is a visual metaphor for the paradoxical nature of all things. The cross is saying that there is *a cruciform pattern to reality*. Reality is not meaningless and absurd (chaos/no patterns/nihilism), but neither is it perfect consistency (rationalism/scientism/fundamentalism). Reality, rather, is filled with contradictions. That's why the medieval Franciscan Saint Bonaventure, and others, called it "the coincidence of opposites" (see Ewert Cousins, *Bonaventure and the Coincidence of Opposites*, Franciscan Herald Press, 1978). Jesus was killed on the collision of cross-purposes, conflicting interests and half-truths that all of life is. The cross was the price that Jesus paid for agreeing to live in a "mixed" world that was both human and divine, bad and good, simultaneously broken and utterly whole. He agreed to carry the mystery and not to demand perfection of God's creation or of God's creatures. He lived fully on the horns of the human dilemma and made it work for us. In fact, he said it is the "only" way. It is in that sense only that Christianity is the "only" way to be saved. We are, indeed, saved by the cross — more than we realized.

Experience of the cruciform pattern to reality always feels like two steps forward and three steps backward. None of us likes it, especially because the three steps backward always feel like dying. Many of us working in the Church right now feel we're in a period of moving the three steps backward, a period of dying. Yet Jesus shows us on the cross that this is the only and constant pattern, and we should not be shocked or surprised by it. The people who *live the contradictions*, in fact, are the saviors of the world. These are the people who are the agents of all true transformation, reconciliation and newness.

People think that you're asking them to compromise on issues or on truth when you talk this way. They will call you a moral relativist or something that sounds dangerous, which seems to be what they thought of Jesus. I want to say this very strongly: That's a smoke screen. That's a diversionary tactic, even if unintentional. This labeling is a way to avoid the horns of the dilemma, to deny the clearly paradoxical nature of almost everything.

We are so hesitant to live with "the scandal of particularity," the primary pattern in the biblical revelation. As soon as you start to discern a clear pattern, the Bible makes an exception to it. I'm not talking about compromising on issues, because I do think society has to decide what is acceptable behavior and what is not. I'm talking about compromising on ego, on which nobody wants to compromise. People say they do not want to give way on important moral issues, but far too often they don't want to give way on the ego's need to be right, superior and in control. This mimics that "original sin," described as a "desire to be like God" and daring to eat the apple of the tree of the knowledge of good and evil. It's the human unwillingness to live in a broken world. In the illusion of an unbroken world, we do not have to rely upon grace, mercy and forgiveness, we do not need to be "saved."

Yet if God does not make exceptions, all of us are in trouble. The evil people I've met in thirty years of priesthood are always absolutely certain they're right. They suffer no self-doubt. They are certain they have the whole truth. But, fortunately, I've been blessed to meet many holy people, too. When you meet a holy person there is a very different aroma, a very different energy, a very different taste and smell. They want to do God's will, they seek to please God. But like Thomas Merton at the end of his life, they are saying, "I don't know if I've ever done your will, all I know is that I want to do your will. I'm not certain I'm pleasing you. All I know is that I desire to please you." And that very desire is itself a gift of God. Not much to brag about in being human!

Who of you can say with total certitude that you know you're doing God's will? I don't any day of my life, and it's very unsatisfying. That's what it means to "bear the mystery," to hang with Jesus on the horns of the human dilemma, to agree to find God in a clearly imperfect world. We would much sooner have certitudes, we would much sooner have order and control and know who the good guys are and who the bad guys are. We don't want to hang in this ambiguous, compromised place with Jesus. Most would prefer dogma and perfectly objective morality to biblical faith any day. Certitude allows you to predict and control outcomes, and to justify rewards and punishments. That's not all bad. The trouble is that it is not the message that shouts from the cross.

Liberals and Conservatives

The more progressive and liberal type of person tends to avoid what I'll call the vertical claims of the gospel. They tend to be a little afraid to talk about transcendence and God. They tend to be a little uncomfortable talking about the wisdom and the importance of the past and of tradition, to know that the truth has always been with us and God has always been with us. Progressive and educated people often love right ideas more than reality in its wounded state. We could call that the vertical line of the cross: transcendence and tradition.

Conservative people tend to avoid the horizontal claims of the gospel. They tend to be afraid of breadth and inclusiveness. They tend to be afraid of mercy and compassion, or any breaking of the rules, particularly rules for group coherence. It's almost as if letting the sinner get in will take away their purity and their worthiness or the identity of their group. They are always circling the wagons around this very fragile God that they have to protect. Often their religion is more tribalism and group belonging than any real search for broad truth. Group belonging takes away a lot of primal shame and fear for most of us.

The liberal types fight structures, authority and self-serving ideologies, not realizing that liberals are usually very individualistic and heady as a result. The liberal types also play the victim whenever it is politically correct to do so. They have a very hard time creating anything that lasts because they are loyal to so little beyond their own experience and their own agenda. Authority is always suspect, and you cannot build positively when you start with suspicion. They also do not pass on their values very well to their children, probably because their values are more against-energy than for-energy. Against-energy does not inspire or convert young idealistic people, political correctness gathers very few, and for a very short time.

The conservative types fight as soon as they have targeted the appropriate sinner, or anyone who threatens their strong control needs. These people expel and reject rather readily, very often creating victims—taking away their own self-doubt. There is often a pseudo innocence in conservative people, which naturally comes from refusing to carry the dark side of reality. This refusal leads to a false moral superiority and a naive certitude, which we call fundamentalism. Conservative types tend to flee from inclusiveness, from depth and from much-needed self-knowledge. They usually have a strong punitive need, perhaps to restore an appropriate sense of an ordered world. There are no free lunches for most conservatives; while liberals are always looking for one for themselves or others.

Together, though, we hang, each with our own needs for conversion. Wherever we find ourselves on the spectrum, we hope we have part of the truth and part of the mystery. But the cross calls all of us to a mystery of transformation. On the cross none of us is in charge, none of us is in control, none of us can possibly understand, just like Jesus himself. On the cross someone else is in control. Someone else is in charge. Someone else understands. Someone else is obviously a much more patient lover than we are.

'They will look on the one whom they have pierced.'
(Zechariah 12:10)

I'd like to end this chapter by offering a prayer that I hope can become your prayer. We will see in a later chapter of this book that Saint Francis of Assisi offered a simple prayer before the crucifix. I would like to offer one for today (albeit wordier than my Father Francis'!). This is a prayer about violence against self, others, the world. I believe that people in flight from themselves are intrinsically violent. People are driven to violence rather than to let themselves know that the death they desire is their own.

Picture yourself before the crucified Jesus and recognize that *he became what we are all afraid of and what we all deny:* nakedness, exposure, vulnerability and failure. He became "sin" to free us from sin, the cosmic Scapegoat who reveals our worst and best souls to those who will gaze long enough. He became the pleading image of what humans do to humans—so we could see it in stark outline, with the curtain of denial withdrawn. He became the crucified so we would stop crucifying. He became the crucified who refused to crucify back, and thus stopped the inevitable pattern of death. Jesus on the cross appeals to all of us to see ourselves—and God—as the victims of human malice.

JESUS SPEAKS: *"My people, I am yourself. I am your beauty. I am your goodness which you are destroying. I am what you do to what you should love. I am what you're afraid of, your deepest and your best and most naked self. Your badness largely consists in what you do to goodness, your own and others—and that is indeed bad. You are afraid of the good. You are afraid of me. You kill what you should love. You hate and fear the very thing that could and will transform you. I am Jesus crucified. I am yourself. And I am all of human history."*

WE SPEAK BACK TO JESUS: *"Lord Jesus crucified, you are my life. And you are also my death. You are my beauty. You are my possibility. You are my full self. You are everything I want, and you are everything I am afraid of. You are everything I desire, and you are everything I deny. You are my outrageously ignored and neglected soul.*

"Lord Jesus, your love is what I most fear. I can't let anybody love me 'for nothing.' I want to be worthy. Unearned intimacy with you or anyone terrifies me. I am beginning to see that I, in my own body, am an image of what is happening everywhere. I want it to stop here, today. I want to stop the violence toward myself, toward the world, toward anybody, toward you, my crucified Lord. I do not ever again need to create a victim of anybody. Neither do I need to play the victim. You have shown me a truly new way.

"You alone, Lord Jesus, refused to be crucifier, even at the cost of being crucified. You never play the victim, you never ask for vengeance, but you only breathe forgiveness. While we on this fearful earth murder, mistrust, attack and hate. Now I see that it is not you that humanity hates; we hate ourselves, but mistakenly kill you. I must stop crucifying your blessed flesh on this earth and in my brothers and sisters, and in every form of life, whether innocent or guilty, worthy or unworthy. We are all your blessed Body, and you have always loved me precisely in my unworthiness. How can I not do the same for others?

"Now I see that you live in me and I live in you. You are inviting me out of this endless cycle of illusion and violence. You are Jesus crucified, you are saving me. In your perfect and patient love you have chosen to enter into union with me. I do not pretend to understand. I can only receive you, trust you and thank you forever. I am your dwelling place. You have chosen to abide with me much more than I have ever chosen you. I am sorry.

"I thank you, Lord Jesus, for becoming a human being so I do not have to pretend or try to be a God. I thank you, Lord Jesus, for becoming finite and limited so I do not have to pretend that I am infinite and limitless. I thank you, crucified God, for becoming mortal so I do not have to try to make myself immortal. I thank you, Lord Jesus, for becoming inferior so I do not have to pretend that I am superior to anyone. I thank you for being crucified outside the walls, for being expelled and excluded like the sinners, so you can meet me where I feel that I am, always outside the walls of holiness.

"I thank you for becoming weak, so I don't have to be strong. I thank you for being willing to be considered imperfect and strange, so I do not have to be perfect and normal. I thank you, Lord Jesus, for being willing to be disapproved of, so I do not have to try so hard to be approved of and liked. I thank you for being considered a failure, so I do not have to give my life trying to pretend I'm a success. I thank

you for being wrong by the standards of religion and state, so I do not have to be right anywhere.

"I thank you for being poor in every way, so I do not have to be rich in any way. I thank you, Lord Jesus, for being all of the things that humanity despises and fears, so I can accept myself and others in you. So I can love in you that very part of me that I most hate.

"Crucified Jesus, I thank you for becoming a human being. I want to love you. I need to love you.

"Lord Jesus crucified, you and I are the same."

They will mourn for [him] as though for an only child.... When that day comes, a fountain will be opened. *(Zechariah 12:10,13:1)*

And when I am lifted up...I shall draw all people to myself. *(John 12:32)*

CHAPTER THREE

Great Awakenings

. . . .

STUDENTS OF HISTORY know that our current thirst for transcendence is not the first in American experience. The United States has seen three spiritual awakenings. These were widespread religious awakenings, or revivals. These awakenings can be criticized on some levels, but they produced a model of social justice and human rights that is still copied worldwide. The first, which historians call The Great Awakening, carried the seeds of the American Revolution and the United States Constitution, and, ultimately, the French Revolution in Europe. Human consciousness and freedoms made a great advance from which we have never withdrawn, at least in principle. It contributed to the modern democratic worldview, "The Declaration of the Rights of Man," the concern for the common person, and laid the foundation for the rights of women and minorities.

The Second Great Awakening, which began at the turn of the nineteenth century, contributed to the eventual abolition of slavery. It was almost as if freedom and human dignity were ideas whose time had come. The soul and the spirit had to be ready for the movement of history. The Second Great Awakening, by calling people to reflect on a transcendent reference point, helped pave the way for a higher morality than mere cultural expedience.

Although we find slavery unthinkable now, it is worth remembering that in much of colonial America it was assumed that inclusion of the institution of slavery was the only way the world had ever been structured. Even in the Bible, Saint Paul, we all know, assumed that the institution of slavery was normal—a good example of how we cannot normally think outside of our own era and culture. Human consciousness has only slowly been ready for the full Christ, for the freedom of the children of God. No surprise that it took us until the 1980's to begin to see the evil of sexism!

The assumption of the necessity of slavery is true even of the very progressive American constitution, which, as we all know, was written with *men* in mind, because women did not have the vote, and *white* men, because black men were slaves. Our founding fathers were well-intentioned and brilliant rationalists, but truly blinded by their own time and culture. We also are blinded by our time and culture, but we cannot yet see it. Surely this is a strong example of how education is not the same as transformation, a theme I will continue to emphasize.

The mind can only take pictures using the film with which it's been loaded. Our inner myths determine what we do and don't pay attention to, what we consider significant and what we ignore. If we had had the openness of ears to hear the full gospel we would have had the openness of eyes to see that slavery and sexism were significant. But our eyes were not ready yet, nor maybe our heart. Nor was history.

In the 1800's, in the wake of this second spiritual awakening, Abraham Lincoln emerged and grew into his greatness. He wasn't always an emancipator, by the way. There must have come an epiphanic moment when he saw slavery was intolerable. The great souls get there first, and eventually it filters down to intermediate souls (most of us), and it takes much longer to get to those who are either uninformed or afraid.

Those who think that the world can only be structured as *they* have known it are the slow learners of history. They fail to realize that their slow learning curve is actually a form of narcissism and also a lack of knowledge. Thus, change comes with great difficulty in human history. God seems to rely on the first group of "great souls" to call the rest of us forward inch by inch, but they normally suffer a great deal for their foreseeing. Most of us like our comfort zones, and take them for granted as we once took the divine right of kings.

The Lincolns of this world are people who have experienced what the New Testament writers termed *metanoia*. The word literally means "a turnaround." It is a fundamental transformation of mind, normally brought about by personal suffering, great awareness or Damascus Road experiences. This reveals an utterly new imaginal world. Until we "imagine" our worldview differently, intellect and will of themselves provide only temporary and often weak change. *Metanoia*, an utter turnaround and seeing with a new mind, is seemingly necessary to transform us personally and to help us transform social structures and institutions. In other words, we are first of all *assumed* to be on a course of ego, narcissism and self-interest, with a what's-in-it-for-me attitude.

Other disciplines might speak of "insight," "eureka moments," "flow," "peak experiences," but *metanoia* is always known to be a kind of grace from nowhere. The recipients always know for sure that it is an utterly unearned gift. If they don't, they are destroyed by their own *hubris*, or pride. The biblical tradition would say that this turnaround is entirely dependent upon an experience of The Absolute. Afterwards, we know at least three things at a deep level: God is good, the world is good and I am good. That is all we need in order to begin. We then have an utterly grounded imaginal consciousness, and fear has been foundationally overcome. Our psyche is no longer based in the small self but in the Great Self, the Christ Self. People like Lincoln, Harriet Tubman and some abolitionists represented this second awakening. It is embarrassing how absent the mainline Churches are during this period. Catholics were still building separate churches for blacks and whites into the early 1960's in some parts of the South! Claims to orthodoxy become very weak when there is almost no orthopraxy.

The third awakening was not so long ago. It was the stirring that led to the labor and civil-rights reforms of the mid-twentieth century. It predisposed American Catholics for the reforms that would come with the Second Vatican Council (1962-65). It gave us the beginnings of what I call "the bias toward the bottom." We can only realize how significantly our thinking has changed back to biblical thinking (where the victims were always the heroes) when we remember that most of human history has idealized kings, money, nobility, fame and power (the bias toward the top).

The Security to Be Insecure

At the time of the Second Vatican Council, in the early 1960's, we Catholics were very self-confident. All indicators of numbers, vocations, money, influence were positive and growing. There was no reason to reform or self-criticize. Our identity was clear, our boundaries were clear, our sense of the absolute was grounded and founded. We knew who we were and, ironically, we were therefore free to criticize ourselves, even from the very top.

The ability to self-criticize and own your own dark side is a clear sign of health and interior freedom. A historian of social change once told me that Vatican Council II was one of the very few times in all of human history that a strong institution reformed itself from the top— when it didn't have to and wasn't forced to. That's a rather strong sign of the presence of God's Spirit.

Today I see in the Roman Church at the higher levels little ability to be self-critical. At this time we feel that we have lost our boundaries in relation to secular culture, and we are trying to shore them up by insisting that we're always right and have the full and total picture. This is called a "siege mentality," and always emerges when a group has lost its former influence and feels that it is under attack.

We are all caught in these bigger *zeitgeists* ("the spirit of an age"). Every age has been. It is almost heroic to live above them, and you never really know if you are. Yet, the person with a great soul is one who moves others toward the future with compassion and confidence — not judgment, paranoia or accusing. We were very happy as Catholics when John Paul II set a new tone in Jubilee Year 2000 and publicly admitted and asked forgiveness for many of the historic sins of Roman Catholicism. It seemed to give permission at all lower levels for honesty and humility about the Church. This might well signal a new beginning.

John Paul II is surely one of these great souls on many levels. His tragic flaw might well be that he does not often trust anyone else to be a great soul or to initiate the grand gesture except himself. He can be ecumenical, but we at the lower levels must exclude even other Christians from the table; he can make major political statements, but other bishops and priests, like the 1980 martyr Archbishop Oscar Romero, are given no support when they do the same. It almost feels a bit schizophrenic, but the issues are so enormous today that only time will prove where wisdom lies (see Matthew 11:19).

But finger-pointing is usually just an avoidance of our own transformation. To continue to move forward calmly, with joy and confidence is probably as clear a sign of God's presence as I can imagine. It is also somewhat rare. But those who can do so are the people who will reconstruct. These are the people who will lead us into God's future. These are the people worth listening to.

Dom Helder Camara, the Archbishop of Recife in Brazil, continued to live and preach with joy and confidence even after his seminary for the poor was undone by a later Vatican appointment. Most women foundresses of religious communities spent much of their life being opposed by bishops and Roman congregations, yet they humbly moved forward with what they know God called them to do. These kinds of fire-tried saints will always win the day for God.

A Sense of History

One of the greatest qualities we must bring to the present malaise, the present dilemma, is a sense of history, a sense that we've been here before. We've seen the overly romantic and the overly rational before. Those extremes have been interwoven throughout history. During the best of times, they've balanced each other. We're not in that balance now: We're either cheaply romantic (most media and liberals), or cheaply rational (many conservatives and fundamentalist religions). We're not open, by and large, to great spirituality or to dealing with things holistically and historically. We just react.

Healthy religion—which profits both the individual and the society—will be both romance *and* reason, faith *and* intelligence, symbol *and* science, experience *and* essence. See Richard Tarnas's masterpiece overview of Western thought: *The Passion of the Western Mind* (Ballantine Books, 1993). Tarnas sees our entire history of philosophy as a balancing act, a pendulum swing between the rational and the romantic. Seldom does it achieve a balance between the two.

Strangely enough, the present liberal-conservative split in the Catholic Church is a mishmash of both on both sides. Conservatives romantically hold onto essence, while being very rational about experience; liberals rationally hold on to experience, while being very romantic about essence. That tells me they both have a kind of truth and wholeness, but are each usually incapable of self-criticism, and incapable of appreciating the other.

Yet, in the midst of this confusion, people of true greatness are emerging, probably sometimes *because* of the confusion and darkness. Their emergences are isolated, individual phenomena, and in my experience, cannot be identified with any one group or religion. As always, the Spirit cannot be controlled and "blows where it pleases" (John 3:8). Jesus is just too much for any one group of us. How good it is to accept that. What a burden off our backs, our judgments, our inflated expectations of everything. Now only God needs to be God.

Many of our social institutions, particularly, government, law, education, the Church, the military, family and marriage have been roundly discredited in the last fifty years. Each one is its own sad story of lost authority and focus. Unfortunately, this leaves only the media and the business world to communicate daily meaning for most people! Now that is scary—and probably this is the first time in human history that we have tried to carry society on two such tiny and fragile shoulders. It is certain to produce fragile people and a very unstable society.

The traditional institutions of our culture are feeling impotent and incapable of communicating believable patterns of wisdom and truth. Lacking authority and credibility, they do not have the power to lead or guide us. We don't give power to them, and they don't have the consensus or the confidence to take it. The Vietnam War, Watergate and the Clinton-Starr impeachment debacle have made us cynical about government and the military; the O. J. Simpson trial and the famous "Twinkie verdict," in which a voluntary manslaughter verdict was passed down for the killings of a San Francisco mayor and a supervisor, made us cynical about the legal-judiciary system; both Catholic and Evangelical fundamentalism, plus the sexual scandals of the clergy, have made us cynical about religion. Our universities do not make us into universal people, but instead have become mostly job-preparation mills. At the personal level, our individualism and narcissism have made the skills needed for marriage and family rare.

This power and confidence vacuum has opened the door for the far right to seize and exploit the language of religion and God—which they have done. The televangelist phenomenon both within Evangelical Protestantism and pious Catholicism is in great part, I believe, the fault of the liberal establishment in this country, which refuses even to acknowledge Transcendence or Tradition in any serious way, forcing an overreaction on the other side. Both sides righteously point to their opposite extremes to justify their own positions. True greatness never emerges in such periods, I am told. We spend too much time putting out fires, attacking and protecting ourselves to get on to intelligence and mysticism. What is lost is the healthy middle where the romantic and the rational can coexist. And that is a big loss.

When you take an extreme position, you take part of the responsibility for pushing people to the opposite extreme. I see, for example, in my own small world, many young priests, laity and new bishops to whom I find it very hard to relate. They seem to me rather rigid, ideological and doctrinaire. Yet when I talk to them personally, I can see them living in fear of the judgments of the feminists and the attacks of the liberals. I can see that they have been hurt by such attacks. We all go to a place where we can feel safe.

When you do not feel safe or secure or "at home," you naturally take a strong stance to define yourself. Unfortunately you are in a corner that you cannot get out of and where others cannot get to you. That's not a very good position from which to proclaim the great Good News. Of course, conservatives push progressives to the same reactionary position by their seeming worship of authority and order as ends in themselves. To educated people, most traditionalists appear to have no interest in honest history or critical thinking, but only in soft piety and propaganda passing for religion. So the liberals get out their information, statistics and scholarship and use it to dismiss the conservatives as promoters of romantic rubbish. The trouble is that both are somehow right.

Stephen Carter is saying the same in his fine book, *The Culture of Disbelief*. He makes the point that the liberal establishment of this country must recognize that it has unwittingly allowed for the ascendancy of the far right by its own nihilism, its throwing out of all boundary markers, its thinking that history began yesterday with us, its stomping on the needed traditions and "romantic" rituals of people. Progressive folks have been far too rational and correct about the needs of the soul.

Can we take responsibility for the fact that we push people to those extremes when we do not stand in the compassionate middle? I think of how often during my talks someone raises a hand and says, "I disagree with what you just said." Eight times out of ten they did not hear what I said. Normally, they don't have the humility to ask in a non-accusatory way: "Did I hear you correctly in saying…?" or "What do you mean when you say…?" The assumption is seldom that *they* could have heard me wrong. The assumption is usually that *you* are wrong. Such a mentality never encourages dialogue or mutuality. Unfortunately, my response too often suffers because of the negative energy generated. I am then defensive, or bite my tongue to control my own judgments or desire to attack back. The result is a half response, at best, because the environment is not safe and congenial.

Our assumption is usually that "I did understand you. I know your motivation. I know what you're trying to say, and I therefore have the need and right to attack you." Normally, neither of us grows or expands in such a context. The truth is not well served, because neither of us feels secure or cared for. Unfortunately, this has become the state of our public discourse, now even in places like the Senate and among major editorial writers. One wonders if we in the Church have shown them an alternative.

Fortunately, there will always be the two out of ten people who have the humility to ask, "Richard, did I understand what you were saying?" Normally then I can clarify, or perhaps admit that I have communicated poorly or am, in fact, wrong. I normally tell people to "listen long enough to me and you won't get too upset." I'll usually balance myself out if they give me enough time. But a lot of people will not give you enough time.

In hostile situations, we find that Jesus either kept silent, reframed the question or put a question back to the speaker. He knew that one never wins when someone has a predisposition toward resentment or a desire to shame you. In such encounters, whatever you say will be turned against you. We have all been in such fruitless and impossible conversations. No one wins.

But that is the way the ego likes to work. Opposition gives you a sense of standing for something, a false sense of control and power. Compassion and humility don't give you a sense of control or psychic comfort. You have to let go of your moral high ground and hear the ten percent truth that the other person is perhaps saying. Compassion and dialogue are essentially vulnerable positions. If you are into control and predictability, you will seldom descend into the weakness of listening or the scariness of dialogue. You will not only be incapable of hearing others, but you will also be incapable of hearing God. How we do anything is usually how we do everything. If we spend all day controlling and blocking others, why would we change when we kneel to pray?

Faith, frankly, demands *faith*—not proof, certitude, predictability, control or the comforts of authority assuring us that we are always right. Our temptation is often to create a non-relational Christianity and non-relational leadership styles, so we can have all the bases covered by custom and statute, and don't ever have to enter into the scandal of particularity. Prayer, perhaps more than anything, is the school of relationship and particularity. We should be the experts in these areas—if we are people of prayer.

Sense of Community

The hunger for meaning and the need for hope that we now have in this deconstructed society cannot be satisfied by mere private choices. This is a real blind spot for most liberals. The issues are too big, and we cannot stand against such a dominant cultural collapse alone. Corporate evil can only be overcome by corporate good. For this reason, and many others, I'm very happy to see the growth of small groups in our Church and in our society.

As we have said since the early days of the New Jerusalem Community in Cincinnati, "you cannot think yourself into a new way of living, but you must live yourself into a new way of thinking." It is lifestyle choices that finally change us and allow us to see in new ways. We have to create structures and institutions that think and, therefore, act differently. We have no past evidence to prove that gospel individuals *alone* can fully exemplify the Reign of God. This is the Church's own form of individualism, while it often condemns individualism in the world. Until we question our very lifestyle nothing truly new is going to happen. Or, as Jesus put it in perfect metaphor: put "new wine into old wineskins" and both will be lost (see Mark 2:22). That's a rather clear statement about the need for gospel structures to nurse gospel individuals. Up to now, we have largely tried to evangelize individuals, while the structures have remained Roman empire, monarchical and unaccountable. "Put new wine in fresh wineskins, and both are preserved" (Matthew 9:17).

Perhaps that is why Jesus does not directly take on social reform. Instead he preaches a life of simplicity and nonviolence that is simply *outside* the system of power, money and control. More than directly fighting the system, *he ignores it* and builds an alternative worldview where power, prestige and possessions are not sought or even admired. Such withdrawal of allegiance is finally the most subversive act possible because the powers that be can no longer control you either positively or negatively (by getting you to react against them). You are no longer inside their reward and punishment system. Maybe that is why mystics, saints and hermits so infuriate the body politic. They ignore the whole thing and build an alternative set of loyalties.

Good Tradition

My brother and sister-in-law have similarly set their family outside the mainstream in buying a house on the same street as her family, and saying, "We are going to raise our kids with a different set of values." When I saw my nephews and their cousins a few weeks ago, I said, "They are different, they really are different." They bring their dogs over for me to bless them. They have no embarrassment in talking about Church or even calling me "Father." Now some would say this is old-fashioned and patriarchal. But when I see that the alternative is cynicism and sarcasm about almost everything, a calm world of mutual respect starts looking pretty beautiful. They are proud of being Catholic, they carry none of the shame that many young Catholic kids have. They were so excited that a priest was in the block for a week! So I was blessing animals and sick people all week. To these folks it's still an enchanted universe, filled with communion and mystery. If religion does not give us that sense of belonging to a sacred world of meaning, it is pretty useless. If you see the world as blessed, then you want your dog in on it, too!

When staying at my brother's house, I observe a world where voices are rarely raised and where the parents and children talk to one another with mutual respect. I don't think we sophisticated folks need to assume that they are all repressed and "in denial." The people I meet who are not cynical are normally people who hold more conservative values—or progressive people who also have a deep spirituality. They are still proud of being whatever they are, and do not waste most of their life debunking the only life that they have. There are always some stable *givens* in their lives, and they do not need to hold them up for daily critique.

Perhaps, like my brother and sister-in-law, they wouldn't think of missing Mass on Sunday. The sacramental symbols and the feast days of the Church are an active part of their life and their week. This gives the children, especially, a sacred and safe world within which they can grow—almost endlessly and almost effortlessly. I know because I had such a world myself, in somewhere-over-the-rainbow-Kansas where I grew up in those safe idyllic years after World War II. Ironically, this prepared me for a world much larger than Kansas. What a paradox!

It seems we have to *begin* conservative—with clear boundaries, identity and a sense of respect for our reality. Then, and only then, can we move out from that strong center according to our education and experience. I really do not know any other way that works for the human soul. You cannot begin aimless, reactionary and picking up pieces on your own. If you do, you have the extreme handicap of beginning at *zero,* which I don't think God ever intended for the individual. That's the necessary and good meaning of Tradition. We were meant to be parts of communities of custom where some of the problems have already been named and resolved for us, even if we still have to do it our own way.

The normal pattern that I find in mythology and story is that the healthy person always begins with idealism, heroism, black-and-white worldviews, and then moves toward nuance, compassion, exception, patience, tolerance and wisdom. We now have it absolutely backwards: People begin with no boundaries or identity, and then overreact by the middle of life and need all kinds of fundamentalist certitudes, clarity, order and absolute authority! I see this especially at the jail with many who wasted their early years on "drugs, sex and rock and roll," and now fight about religious platitudes with absolute arrogance and ignorance—a toxic combination! This is probably predictable for many baby boomers and those who came later. It does not bode well for the future of religion or even for the future of intelligent conversation.

To live with healthy Tradition is not an individual experience—it is a communal one. Perhaps this is why Catholicism emphasizes liturgy so much. It is the one thing that pulls us into a communal space where we can ask different questions, look at reality from a different perspective and be told different truths than the small truths of the "private I."

The endless telling of "this is me" stories eventually becomes self-validating, self-imprisoning and, frankly, boring. Personal anecdotes become too small and aimless unless they are a part of some larger life narratives. That is the genius of family stories, mythologies and the biblical mind.

Reconstruction

When we speak of rebuilding, we're talking in great part about the rebuilding of a public world, public institutions and public forums. Attitude change is only a beginning, but it is still too privatized. We start with personal conversion, but we have to move toward structures that can allow that vision to be shared with other people and to be passed on to the next generation. As I said before, conservative people tend to be better at this than progressives, who build few lasting structures. This is probably why most religion is inherently conservative. The genius is to distinguish between healthy conservatism and mere self-serving maintenance of status-quo structures. You can look conservative and merely be afraid of larger truth, imagination, intelligence, risk and, finally, faith. God deserves more than that, I think. True Traditionalists are not always conservative by temperament. True Traditionalists just know that there are some old boundary markers that were put there for a reason.

Ralph Waldo Emerson, the great American essayist, said "nothing great is ever achieved without enthusiasm." What a deconstructed culture lacks, because of its deep cynicism and pessimism about reality, is a basic confidence and enthusiasm that is necessary to start almost anything. You cannot begin with mere criticism or againstness—or it finally turns against your own group (witness the later stages of most angry revolutions, even much of the work of the "Protest"ant Reformation, and the new Catholic reactionaries who are already splitting over who is more orthodox). The brittle or negative personality finally breaks against itself and its own type. You can only build on life, and not on death.

I will always cherish my early years among the youth of the New Jerusalem community in Cincinnati. If we were nothing else we were enthusiastic! There was belief, there was trust, there was positive energy—everything was not immediately critiqued, analyzed and called into question. I always said, "Let's be free to say yes before we say no." Over the years my appreciation for how profound that truth is has deepened. The AA saying that "analysis is paralysis" indicates a learned pattern that many educated people need to unlearn.

Most of us are not free to say yes before we say no. Our first response is normally "no": "I don't trust that. I don't like that. I don't agree with that." The word *enthusiasm* (*en-theos* in Greek) means "filled with God." I'm not encouraging mindless enthusiasm, but the enthusiasm that is based on intelligence and wisdom and that great gift of hope. Hope is a participation in the very life of God. This hope has nothing to do with circumstances or things going well. It can even thrive in adversity and trial. True faith, which always includes hope and love—is a predisposition to yes. And I would say that a foundational *yes* is the most distinguishing element between a secular agenda and one that is guided by the Spirit of Jesus. You can spot the different energy in a moment! "With him it was always Yes, and however many the promises God made, the Yes to them all is in him" (2 Corinthians 1:19, 20). Jesus was a "Yes" man in the deepest meaning of that phrase.

If you came to our Center for Action and Contemplation in New Mexico and saw the staff walking around badmouthing others, or frenetically pushing for their own agenda, you would not think much of us. You would not believe that we were representing the new agenda of God and calling forth a Greater Truth. And you would be right. When you are doing "God's thing," you don't need to push the river. The river is God's unilateral and always reliable love. And that should make our style, even our corporate style, utterly different than that of almost anybody else. You can be positive and even cheerful, because it does not all depend on your getting it right or doing it right. You are merely, as Francis said, "a servant of the Great King."

Stringing Pearls

Once we are critical or educated people, deconstructionism will come naturally to most of us. For some reason, no comes more easily than yes, and is almost the very proof that you are indeed sophisticated. But deconstruction is rather useless without reconstruction, without a positive vision. As we said in Chapter Two, it is the easiest thing in the world to point out what is wrong, who is wrong and to stand on a pedestal of superiority—without *doing* anything positive—or *becoming a positive answer*—ourselves. After you deconstruct, what are you actually *for*? An awful lot of activists on the left and reactionaries on the right have no positive vision, nothing they believe *in*, no one they are in love *with*. They are just overwhelmed with what's wrong, and think that by eliminating the so-called "contaminating element" the world will be pure and right again.

That is the major illusion of people on both left and right. In different ways they are both into a politics of expulsion. It's just the object of their expulsion that is different. One day the mainline Christian movement will itself recognize that Jesus was never into expelling or excluding—only transforming and integrating. In fact, you might say, that for Jesus the very act of expulsion is the problem. He is always sending the lepers and those healed back into the city, back to the priests, out of the cemetery of chains and gnashing of teeth.

We're glad that people are working for justice and peace, we are happy that people are seeking to overcome evil. But problem-solving, punishing offenders and shunning the nonconformists will not of itself create a new vision, a new society. Without a positive vision, the Book of Proverbs says, the people will perish (see 29:18). What the gospel, what true religion, what true mythology gives us is a cosmic and positive vision inside of which the soul can live safely. That's the only place from which lasting change ever comes. Jesus' word for that totally positive vision—not against anybody or expelling anything—is "the Reign of God." He *includes* ("forgives") sinners instead of excluding or scapegoating them. In that light, it is rather amazing that institutional Christianity ever created the very concept of excommunication. Only the individual can do that to himself, and we had best not make it our corporate concern. Hinduism, the oldest religion in the world, has never excommunicated anybody.

"Garbage in, garbage out," the healing professions have been saying. Some people call this phenomenon "karma," or define it as meaning "what you give out is what you will get back." If you build on death, you end up with death. If you build on life, you end up with more of the same, because spiritual gifts increase with usage. A Hasidic master put it best of all: "Rake the muck this way, rake the muck that way, it will still be muck. In the time that I am brooding, I could be stringing pearls for the delight of heaven."

I recently heard Dorothee Soelle, the German theologian. She said, "We are spiritual orphans in the West today. We have lost access to our own spiritual roots, the only ones that we have." She's right: The young people of Germany, she said, travel the world to find their own spiritual heritage. They can't find it at home anymore because everybody has rejected their own tradition after it failed them so miserably in the Nazi era.

Aleksandr Solzhenitsyn, the Russian writer, put it even more desperately when he said, "The West is in a state of spiritual exhaustion." It's a telling metaphor. The Western mind refuses to be in awe anymore. It is only aware of what is wrong, and seemingly incapable of rejoicing in what is still "good and true and beautiful." The only way out is a new imagination and new cosmology created by positive God experience. Education, liberal politics, problem-solving, rigid ideology are all finally inadequate by themselves to create cosmic hope and meaning. Only great religion can do that, which is probably why Jesus spent so much of his ministry trying to reform religion. Nothing less will do.

Healthy religion gives you a foundational sense of awe. It re-enchants an otherwise empty universe. It gives people a universal reverence toward all things. Only with such reverence do you find confidence and coherence. Only then does the world become a safe home. Then we can see the reflection of the divine image in the human, in the animal, in the entire natural world—which has now become inherently "supernatural." That is the paradox, and all dualistic language will henceforth fail us. When the divine image is no longer there why should I respect you, or anything? Why should I talk to you with tenderness if you do not reflect the divine image, if you are just another market product?

Humanism is actually a result of the gospel, but it is not the gospel itself, because it refuses the total seeing and foundation for absolute reverence. It tries to obey the Second Commandment without the First, and it is finally inadequate. (Although we must admit that many humanists seem to love their neighbor in practice much better than many professed Christians. God uses all of us as instruments. Christians just have the advantage of knowing they are indeed instruments—and living in that joy now.)

It is, of course, finally the doctrine of the cross which pushes this divine reflection to its utter limits. More than anything else, the cross says that God can and must be seen in all things, but most especially in the seemingly sinful, broken and tragic things. The place of the supposed worst becomes the place of the very best. The mystery of the cross teaches us to be prepared to be surprised about how and where God reveals God's heart. It is beyond our control.

The Sacred Wound

When we lose the reflection of the divine image in all things, I think we're going to disintegrate quickly. The postmodern mind has too little respect (*re-spicere*, "to look again"), too little ability to look again at what it has too easily dismissed. Both superficial science and much secular education have limited themselves to only partial seeing (see the monumental works of spiritual intellectual and writer Ken Wilber in this regard). With too little respect, the postmodern mind won't see all the way through things. It's the same with a lot of therapy and psychology: They're right as far as they go, but they stop too soon. Healthy religion pushes you all the way through. It tells you, "Don't stop with your anger, your disillusionment, your scientific explanation." Deconstruction is only the first stage toward a new reconstruction. The biblical prophets would have called it "the toppling of idols," which rightly precedes the entrance into the temple of the true sacred.

Christianity in its mature forms keeps pushing us toward the necessary tragic: "the folly of the cross," as Paul calls it.

Normally the way God pushes us is by disillusioning us with the present mode. Until the present falls apart, we will never look for Something More. We will never discover what it is that really sustains us. But that dreaded experience is always suffering in some form. All of us hate suffering, yet all religions talk about it as necessary. It seems to be the price of the death of the small self and the emergence of the True Self, when we finally come to terms with our true identity in God. Many Jungians describe this in psychological terms as the "necessary soul suffering" that comes from the death of the ego. Jesus would say, "Unless the grain of wheat dies, it remains just a grain of wheat" (John 12:24). By avoiding this legitimate pain of being human, we sadly bring on ourselves much longer lasting and, often, fruitless pain.

In our men's spirituality work, we call that suffering in its transformed state "the sacred wound," a concept drawn from classical mythology, but also from the Christ story. In mythology the would-be hero is always wounded. The word *innocent* (*innocens*, "not wounded yet") is not a complimentary term in mythology. The *puer* is the young boy who refuses to be wounded, or more exactly, refuses to recognize and suffer the wounds that are already there. He's just going to remain nice and normal, so everybody will accept him. In our culture he might smugly remain white and middle class, healthy, "sinless," Catholic, pretty and happy, maybe even drive a classy car or wear the latest clothing. He refuses to let it fall apart. He refuses to be wounded, much less to allow the humiliating wound to become sacred and sanctifying. Yet, I personally believe that the Gospels are saying there is no other way to know something essential. Allowing our always-unjust wounds to, in fact, become sacred wounds, is the unique Christian name for salvation. *One always learns one's mystery at the price of one's innocence.*

Now if an individual can trust the pain, not get rid of it until s/he has learned its lessons—the suffering can be seen as a part of the Great Pattern, how God is transforming all things. If there is one consistent and clear revelation in the Judeo-Christian Scriptures, it is that the God of Israel is the one "who turns death into life" (see Deuteronomy 32:39, Romans 4:17, 1 Corinthians 1:9). When we can trust the transformative pattern, when we can trust that God is *in the suffering*, our wounds become sacred wounds and the actual and ordinary life journey becomes itself the godly journey, trusting God to be in all things, especially in "his most distressing disguise" of sin and suffering.

Catholics reaffirm this unwelcome truth at the heart of every eucharistic liturgy, knowing how easy it is to forget *the* mystery of faith. Let me personalize it and paraphrase it in this way: "Christ and the soul must die. Christ and the soul must rise. And that pattern must happen many times before we understand it."

Paul states it even more clearly in Galatians:

I have been crucified with Christ [the small and false self must die].... and I live now not with my own life [it feels utterly inadequate and now unnecessary], but with the life of Christ who lives in me [realization of an Indwelling gratuitous Lover]. *(Galatians 2:20)*

The Eastern Tradition called this process by the daring word *divinization*. We still feel presumptuous in claiming such an impossible inheritance. We like to earn things, but an inheritance is only learned, and humbly received.

This classic pattern of transformation into "who we are in God" is called the paschal mystery. And it is the only theme of each and every Eucharist—because it is so necessary to believe, and because we will do anything to avoid it. The liturgy slowly convinces us of who we are, although I have often said at Mass that it is easier for God to convince bread than it is to convince us! Bread knows, wine understands. Humans fight, deny, resist and disbelieve anything they feel unready for or unworthy of. Thus Jesus had to present the gift in the image of a resented banquet in Luke 14:12-24. Paul speaks in the language of free inheritance for those who would prefer to be slaves (Romans 8:14-17). In all cases, it feels like a wounding to our sophisticated soul. For some strange reason, love wounds us and beauty hurts us.

When the wound happens in a secular society like ours, we usually look for an immediate way to resolve it: playing the victim, mobilizing for vengeance (while sometimes calling it "justice"), or looking for someone to blame, or someone to sue! A sacred culture would never bother with such charades and missed opportunities. Rather than a sacred wound, suffering for us often becomes a mere wound and, eventually, an embittering wound. The journey stops there and there's no future. Without the dignifying wound, there is no mystery, no greatness, no soul and surely no Spirit. The theme is so constant in poetry, literature and drama, that one wonders how we could continue to miss it: The wounded one is always the one with the gift; the comfortable one knows nothing.

What we have now in the West, by and large, is embittering wounds. The spiritual "machine" for turning wounds into glory has been lost by a secular people. Yet all the great mythologies and mystics tell us that we *will* be wounded, we *must* be wounded. It is what you do with the wounding that makes all the difference. There is something that you know after having passed through "the night sea journey" (an archetypal theme denoting a necessary trial of the would-be hero) that apparently you can know in no other way.

In classic tragedies, everyone sins and fails, but somehow they retain their human dignity. In classic comedy, everything is fine and dandy, but they all end up looking ridiculous. Life is a divine tragedy much more than a divine comedy, if I can dare to disagree with Dante.

Faith allows you to trust that God is in the suffering and trial: "I thank you, Lord, for what you want to teach me in this." Now you won't say that on the first day, or probably not even on the second, but maybe on "the third day"! Such people are literally indestructible, or in Christian language, "resurrected from the dead." This is one meaning of being "born again" and has more to do with having come through suffering alive and better than an emotional experience after an altar call.

Ancient religions called it "the inexorable wheel," or "the wheel of fortune," the mystery of life and death that just keeps turning. You have to take your time on the down side of the wheel and take your turn on the up side of the wheel and learn in both cycles. That's why Jesus said the rich man could not know what he was talking about (Mark 10:26), because the "rich" man refuses to take his turn on the down side of the wheel. He tries to buy his way out of absurdity, to avoid the essentially tragic nature of human existence by manufacturing a false path of comfort and control. Nothing new happens here. Nothing is transformed. The Holy One is not trusted. The self remains small.

Dying is not extraneous to life; it is a part of the mystery. And you do not understand life until you stand under death. Yet both sides of the mystery must be experienced and trusted. The Eastern religions speak of the yin and yang of things; nature religions simply speak of darkness and light; the Jewish people speak of slavery and deliverance; we Christians speak of death and resurrection. But we are all pointing to God's universal pattern of trust and transformation. This is rightly spoken of as being "reborn," but has less to do with an emotional Church experience than *a realigning life experience.*

Yes, God is dying in all things, but God is risen in all things too. And both at the same time! There is suffering in all things, as the Buddhists so honestly say. There's ecstasy in all things, as the Sufis so honestly say. There are both wild beasts and angels in the wilderness of human life, as the Gospels say (Mark 1:13). People who see "the better angels of our nature" (Abraham Lincoln), while not avoiding "the essentially tragic nature of human existence" (Miguel de Unamuno) are always the seers, the mystics, the prophets, the Great Souls, the fuel that keeps history advancing.

Part of the great mystery of life is that it's just as hard to see the ecstasy and beauty of things as it is to accept the crucifixion of things. Both are the paschal mystery—Christ has died, Christ has risen—and both are an utter act of faith and surrender. In fact, when I see how the negative response comes first to most people, I wonder if the seeing of the Resurrection is not actually the harder act of faith. We note this in all four Gospel accounts, and I think it is more significant than we imagined—not just doubting Jesus' personal resurrection, but equally doubting our own, that of others and the ability of God to turn all human crucifixions into a cosmic resurrection.

Romano Guardini said something that I still don't like and I wish he had not said it, but I know it to be true. He said, "The cross that Christ is often crucified on is the Church itself." It was the high priests and the elders and the scribes who turned Christ over for crucifixion. On the smaller level, it is also our closest friends and partners who often try us the most. Note the necessary betrayals of Peter, Judas. It *had* to happen. (See John 17:11 and Acts 1:16.) I don't fully understand why it is that way, but it seems that the very vehicles that proclaim and promote the Christ mystery in us are also its greatest obstacles!

Yet, this is also a consolation, because the larger Church is only a larger reflection of me. The individual and the corporate Body seem to mirror one another, challenge one another and convert one another. The individual and the corporate Body are "foils" to one another. (A foil is any person or thing, which by strong contrast, underscores or enhances the other.) They are necessary foils for one another, I suspect, although it often seems to work in only one direction. I think the individual believer must also be allowed to challenge the corporate Body to a deeper faithfulness to Jesus.

We shouldn't be too surprised at the common antagonisms within the Church. We always hate truth when it's too close to us. We are always most capable of hating the people who are closest to us. We all know that the greatest antipathies are often between husband and wife, parent and child, Christian and other Christian. The mirror revealing our own shadow is held too close to our face. The Church's closeness to Christ carries with it that same peril. It carries the weight of this great Christ mystery, and it knows what Christ will demand of the soul.

So even though the Church proclaims the Christ, in fact it is afraid of Christ. How could it not be? If we faced up to what Christ is actually saying, we would have to live up to it. So the Christian ego, struggling to survive, blocks and guards against the Great Christ as he comes charging down the field of history. Strange, isn't it? But merely look at our record on slavery, the liberation of human sexuality, authoritarianism, racism, sexism, ecology, the rights of labor, materialism, militarism, non-violence and simplicity. These have not been areas of our strength, yet they follow from the direct teaching of Jesus. We divide over our designated leader, precisely because he *does* have authority in our life, just as children fight and resent their parents. Most of these issues were first recognized as issues by non-believers and then gradually validated as issues by Christian teaching.

Yet we can neither doubt nor deny that the Church still keeps promoting the mystery of Christ, almost in spite of itself. It raises up the sign and symbol so all of us can be seduced and drawn into the crucible of transformation. We fall in love with Jesus and his great gospel, and then spend the rest of our lives being opposed by the very one who gave us the gospel in the first place. Yet it is usually the Great Tradition that gave us the very categories of truth, love and justice that we throw back at that Tradition! People fight Christianity with Christian criteria! People resent the Church with Church categories! So God is winning anyway, and does not seem to care who gets the credit.

It seems unlikely at first, but when I see husbands and wives fighting one another then I understand. You fight the one you love. You fight the love who's closest, who demands everything of you. You fight the love that demands that you love it back. So it doesn't surprise me anymore, although it terribly disappoints me that the Church itself fights and blocks the gospel so much. I had once assumed that the "head office" would naturally be my backup, encouragement and support. Many times it has been, as long as the stretch is not too far. So I am still grateful for this Church, which both mothers me and maddens me. My human mother did the same.

Connecting to the Real World

Today I believe we have failed to produce real spirituality (or real holiness, if you prefer that word) in many adherents of religion. It is not readily apparent that a large percentage of baptized Christians are in love with God or much less "moulded to the pattern of his death" (Philippians 3:11). We've "churched" many people, both good, sincere people and people who simply *like* religious trappings and language. But real transformation into a "new creation" is hardly known to be the agenda. People living "through him, with him, and in him" are much less common than people pursuing a certain kind of positive self-image. The record of religion worldwide is not very good in promoting forgiveness, tolerance, compassion and generosity. I have often said that I would sooner deal with the real sins of people who are living in the-true-self-in-God than the virtues of people who are still living in the false self, which is now religious. Such virtue the world can do without.

There are three common stances in religion: (1) the old self on the occasional new path, (2) the new self on the new path and (3) the new self on the occasional old path. The first is by far the most common and the most disappointing. The second is the perfect saint who hardly ever exists. The third is the real arena of growth and salvation for almost all human lives that I have ever met. It is what the New Testament still calls "the saints."

Today in many cases we have a lot of ideological hysteria and junk religion—on both the left and the right (New Age and Jesus Seminar fundamentalism among the liberals; papal idolatry and nonhistorical orthodoxy among the conservatives). It's similar to junk food because it only satisfies enough to settle the momentary dust, but does not really feed the intellect or heart. Junk religion is usually characterized by fear of the present and fear of the future (which is really fear of God). What you hear when people have really met God is that there is no fear of the present because it is always full, there's no fear of the future because God's in charge, there is no fear of the past because it has been healed and forgiven. Then people do not use God to avoid reality or to fabricate a private self-serving reality, but they let God lead them into the fullness of Reality. Not *away from* dilemmas and paradoxes, but right *onto the horns of the human dilemma*! (See Michael Dwinell's especially fine book, *God-Birthing*, Liguori Press, 1994.)

Whatever reconstruction we're going to do cannot be based on fear and cannot be based on reaction—even reaction against junk religion. It has to be based on *a positive and fully human experience* of God as a loving Presence. When you see a religion that is preoccupied with security, fear, maintaining a positive self-image, when religion is punitive, and thinks that it can lead you to God by threat and coercion, you know it is junk religion. True religion is ready to let God be in charge, and to let God lead us into a new future that we do not yet understand—and no longer even need to understand.

The greatest Catholic moral theologian of this century, Bernard Häring, said that many of the patterns and practices of present institutional religion reveal what he daringly called "behavioral atheism." We only need to be "control freaks," when we don't believe that God is in charge or when we can't trust God to be in charge. Practical atheism is probably the most common way that we all live. I know I do most days of my life.

So what must we let go of? Anxiety would be the natural starting place. I admit that takes a lot of letting go—and it takes all of our life to begin to get there. In fact, we cannot *get* there at all—we are led, seduced and drawn by the endless subterfuges of God. God, like a thief, steals our addictions from us. We can go back and work for justice, peace and truth, but it will be a new self doing it, and, we hope, in a new and creative win/win way.

Rupert Sheldrake speaks of "transformative traditionalism," as opposed to cheap traditionalism that often keeps us inside of our comfort zones under the rubric of loyalty and orthodoxy. The patterns of how humans enter into relationship and destroy relationship are always the same, transformative traditionalism says. Maybe we've progressed in terms of science and medicine and technology and building nice homes. But there's no reason for us to believe that the soul is any wiser than it was in any previous century. The recurring patterns in transformative Tradition are always patterns of growth, change and repentance—which actually increase anxiety; and not just patterns of "repetition" to take away our anxiety. Transformative traditionalism leads you right into your anxieties, so you have to meet God, change—or die. The old-fashioned words for that are heaven, purgatory and hell.

The Vital Information Needed to Survive

I've been recommending to a lot of people Bill McKibben's book, *The Age of Missing Information* (Plume, 1993). McKibben takes one day watching ordinary prime-time television in America and records all twenty-four hours of it on his VCR—everything that comes across on cable TV. In the even chapters in his book he analyzes what this is teaching him about the nature of reality.

Then he takes twenty-four hours sitting alone on the top of a mountain in the Adirondacks in New York. In the alternate chapters he teaches what he learned in that 24-hour period. His conclusion is that the vital information that human beings need to survive spiritually is learned more in silence than on any possible television show. It feels like a secular call to contemplation.

He says that we're being taught not just useless information on TV, but very real patterns which numb and destroy and make impossible the vital wisdom that we need. TV is actually counterproductive—not only in its content but in its form. For example, the very style of MTV and most commercials teach us to be satisfied with strobe light snapshots of life, with no beginning, middle or end, no continuity or purpose beyond the stimulating images themselves. In MTV-land there's simply episodic meaning. We are back into deconstruction, a discontinuous world.

It is not good for the soul to be subjected to thousands of images that hint at sexuality and hint at violence, but without consequences. There's no character development, there is no continuity in relationship, there's no real suffering in the shootings, no price or meaning to that sexual gesture. That's a lie about the nature of reality, which is probably a simple definition of evil. We are not being served well by mere stimulation. All the great religions actually taught means of *under-stimulation* as the primary spiritual discipline.

Some of you might think the above is overstated. But now I know why some couples have even gone so far as to take the TV out of their house. They're desperate to re-find meaning. They're desirous of reconstructing the world on some old and also new levels. For the most part, I see conservatives avoiding transformation and I see progressives avoiding traditions. All of us lose "the vital wisdom that is necessary for the soul to survive."

Eucharist and Family Meal as Reconstructive Ritual

No group of people has any influence on history unless it has common rituals that name and demarcate the seasons and the meanings of their lives, both individually and together.

There certainly has been no symbol for Catholic Christianity that has been more central than the celebration of the Eucharist. *Eucharistein* is the Greek word meaning "thanksgiving." Thus the Eucharist is a thanksgiving meal. The early Christians combined the weekly Jewish Scripture service with the Jewish Passover meal into one meal intended as a symbol of universal table fellowship. In light of that, it is disappointing whenever it has become a symbol of ethnicity, worthiness or group membership and loyalty.

Jesus' most common image for what he was doing in his three years of public ministry is the image of a wedding banquet. When he talked about the banquet, when he talked about the feast, it was always a feast of an endless table that had room for the outcasts, room for those who were not inside, that were somehow considered the outsiders. (See, for example, all the rule-breaking meals in Luke's Gospel, particularly Luke 14:1-24. Or see Matthew 22:9-10, "Go to the crossroads and invite everyone you can find to the wedding"—good and bad alike!)

In my experience of priesthood, Mass has been most effective and most exciting when the celebration is most clear and prayerful. When you can get down to the bare symbols, they're primal, compelling and universal. As Gandhi said, "The world is so hungry that God could only come into the world in the form of bread." We so long for joy that God even risked coming into the world in the form of intoxication, that risky thing called wine. While its excess has caused so much suffering, for most of us wine nonetheless offers conviviality, communion, freedom and even joy. The Eucharist, the sharing of the bread and wine, is a meal of communion. And if that were not enough, all the necessary symbols of transformation, C.G. Jung said, are contained within the Catholic Mass.

During these times of cultural transition, I see the priesthood being diminished and even disappearing in so many places. What is the message of God to our Church in all of this? (I have to assume that God is doing this.) Maybe at this time we are being led back to our original Jewish roots. In Judaism, most of the major rituals, most of the major feast days are not celebrated in the synagogue or the Temple, but around the family table. The mother and the father are clearly the priests of the meal. The sacred is located in the domestic and everyday world.

In a certain sense, some of our current confusion about the priesthood seems misplaced or even unnecessary. One way or another, the great celebration of the Eucharist, where families from various households gather together, will be maintained, perhaps on the great feast days and in local churches. Maybe priests need to be more like overseeing bishops, and the heads of families need to be more like priests! This will never please those with primary managerial concerns, but it will very much please those with concern for depth, family and the power of the personal. "Location, location, location," the motto of successful entrepreneurs, makes a lot of sense spiritually, too.

We must relocate religion in the universal and ubiquitous home, or we will continue to have a church of highly passive and even infantile levels of commitment. We priests must be humble enough to see that, with the best of intentions, we have castrated the historical spiritual leadership of the male, the father, the parents themselves. We moved religion to a level of organization where it was largely anonymous, impersonal, unaccountable and therefore ineffective for most people. No wonder the storefront and evangelical churches keep growing, while we retain an overwhelming amount of members who want "nothing more than to be left alone," to use Cardinal Newman's sad phrase.

We need to nurture the roles of spiritual mothers and spiritual fathers in our homes. At our everyday tables the Lord is present, after all. Home meals ought to be faith-filled meals. Maybe God is telling us something in our current shortage of priests—maybe God is calling his Church to resanctify the home and to relocate the ordinary feasts there, much as the weekly Sabbath meal and even the Passover meal are for Jews. Here the parents preside.

I don't think we need a lot of "middle management" when we have true spirituality. The product and the customer have to be kept close, immediate and personally owned. The whole thing has to move down one full level, in my opinion. We need to rediscover the sanctity of the natural family as the basic institution of society. When we rediscover the sacred *there*, our fathers will know the priesthood of their fatherhood and our mothers will know the priesthood of their motherhood.

I use the word *priesthood* intentionally, because priesthood simply means the one who names the connection between the transcendent world and this world. If you make that connection, you're a priest. This is the priesthood that all Christians are called to by virtue of their being baptized as "priest, prophet and king" or "priestess, prophetess, and queen." We institutional priests far too often connect people with Church more than with a daily spiritual life. It is the common substitution of the vehicle for the journey itself, the menu for the meal itself. As my friend Paula D'Arcy so well says, "God comes disguised as your life."

We must be honest and say that the role of spiritual leadership has been abdicated by many Christian and Catholic mothers and fathers, handed over to the hierarchical priesthood and to ordained ministers. In fact we Catholics have narrowed our understanding of priesthood so much that we only see priesthood in our ordained priests. Holy "Orders" are good and essential, but they must be balanced by some "Holy Non-Orders." It is not as if our success has been so overwhelming that we cannot imagine doing it better.

Yes, there will always be a place for classic cathedral feast-day liturgy.

But I would almost see it moving in the two directions: the great magnificent feast and the almost daily or weekly family feast around the family table.

Recovering the sacred character of the family meal is a reconstructive act that is close at hand. I'm not talking about the whipping off of the classic family mealtime grace, "Bless us, O Lord, and these Thy gifts, which we are about to receive from thy bounty through Christ our Lord, Amen." (I knew a family that used to practice how fast they could say it just to shock guests!) I'm talking about more than the simple grace at meals, perhaps a reading now and then, perhaps a guided conversation on a specific topic—almost anything, where the father and mother take on their role as mentors, guides, spiritual leaders of the whole.

Rituals create families, in a sense. Any parent knows that when you do something at least two years in a row the little ones wait for it for the third year. Children have a natural sense of timing, ritual, seasons and feasts. Ritual is the key to resacralizing the home. I don't want to suggest the particular rituals that a family should name and claim. Certainly each family has its own customs, and there are a number of religious resources that suggest new family rituals for those who need ideas. I'm just saying that we need to take this whole area more seriously, especially during the current cultural crisis. It could well be enough to hold our culture and society together, because it starts with the basic social building block of meaning, the natural family. We jumped it up a level to the spiritual family before the smaller unit was evangelized.

We must rediscover the Eucharist—and indeed our own family meals—as feasts of God's magnanimity, as celebrations of God's gracious givenness to this work-a-day world. We must trust that the material world can be an adequate sign of the spiritual world, in things as ordinary as bread and wine, as common as the family meal. We must see their sacramental nature. Priestly sacraments are overdone when they lose a true sacramental understanding of reality. We do not have to leave the ordinary world to find the holy. We are doing God no favor to keep "the holy" under our jurisdiction.

There were two places where I have found Catholic prayer life to be located in the home, around family altars and family prayer: the Philippine Islands and Kerala in South India. In both places, I met some of the most fervent and in-depth Catholics in the world. The head of the Capuchin Mission Office said some years ago that he could make a statistical case that where Mass has been offered most scrupulously are the very countries where the faith is most weak and passive. (See *The Coming of the Third Church*, Walbert Buhlmann, O.F.M.Cap., Orbis, 1976.) That is scary, even if it is only half true. We can do better, and I am convinced that we will. History is forcing us. God is therefore inviting us.

CHAPTER FOUR

Transformation

· · · · · · · · · ·

ONE WOULD THINK that the unexpected brings the most stress to our lives. But psychologists say that planned change is even more disruptive than unplanned change. Somehow things that just happen are seen as "acts of God." We can fight them, ignore them or accept them. But we know we can't fix them or change them, so after initial shock or even disappointment, we find the energy to deal with them. We find the grace to rise to the occasion. But when we think there's some malicious or lesser mind at work, or that we could have changed it by wile or guile, we fight it, fret over it and never stop fussing, at least internally. That's stress.

For the past thirty years we've been experts at *planning* change. That is a new phenomenon for the most part. Unfortunately, it has now become a mindset and a way of life. We think we can do it and that we *ought* to be doing it. That's not to say that some of the changes we've brought about in Church and society weren't good and necessary, but I think we have paid a large price internally for such a Promethean, daringly original, self-image. For the most part, we can no longer just "let it be." We are now natural fixers, changers, adjustors, constant engineers of our own reality. It makes for a very different kind of soul. It develops what I call "the calculative mind," as opposed to the goal of all mature spirituality: the contemplative mind.

The attitude that is needed for deep and panoramic seeing is not a fixing, calculating stance, but much more an attitude of listening and trusting and waiting. It is the only way "to get out of the way" with our judgments, control mechanisms and personal opinions. Maybe that's why Jesus says we are saved by faith, by trusting and surrendering instead of pushing and trying, by passion ("suffering of" reality) rather than deliberate action. Interestingly, we say we are saved by the passion, death and resurrection of Jesus—all things that are done to him more than anything he does.

It seems that the human person needs an Absolute outside of itself. Have you noticed how much the enthusiastic types on television or radio use the word *absolutely*? Even when they're talking about an exercise machine! In an age when we have no real absolutes, the whirling mind and emotions look for something to settle upon to take away their anxiety. We seem to need an outer reference point to stop the vertigo of our own imagination, and the tyranny of having to make constant choices. We seem to need some kind of god to serve as a centerpiece. I will create an absolute for myself to justify and settle my choices! My football team, my marriage, my religion, my land, my theory, my self-image, my rights, my exercise machine, anything at all. Just give me something to wrap my thoughts and feelings around for awhile, something outside of myself—an idea, an event, a person, a project—to free me from the boredom and tyranny of myself! *It works* and gives one a settled sense of purpose and direction. Without it, we find it very hard to live with our own mind and emotions.

The idea is not wrong, just misplaced. The only real issue, of course, is to find an absolute that really has *some* Absolute character to it. That is probably the difference between a wise person and a merely opinionated or driven person. Wisdom knows what is worth worshiping and honoring; the rest of us will settle for anything to get us through the next conversation. I believe that everybody has faith in something to survive, even if it is faith in cynicism. We all find something to lean on, and false gods do work for short periods. But have no doubt, we all find some absolute to whirl around, even if it is an absolute opinion that there is no God.

I use the concepts of faith and the contemplative mind almost interchangeably. For me they are the same reality, both describing the trustful and God-centered way that we can allow ourselves to be used. In this "different mind" we do not so much try to change reality or others, as allow ourselves to be changed, so that we can be *useable for God*. It is not so important *what* we do now—as *the who that is doing it*. This is crucial, and is at the heart of what we mean by that amorphous word *holiness*. There is a radically transformed experience of the *I* when we are "holy," both within yourself and by those who observe you. The private "I" has been transformed into a Larger Self, that believers would call God. "I live no longer not I..." (see Galatians 2:20).

Belly of the Whale

The word *change* normally refers to new beginnings. But transformation, the mystery we're examining, more often happens *not when something new begins but when something old falls apart*. The pain of something old falling apart—chaos—invites the soul to listen at a deeper level. It invites, and sometimes forces the soul to go to a new place because the old place is falling apart. Most of us would never go to new places in any other way. The mystics use many words to describe this chaos: fire, darkness, death, emptiness, abandonment, trial, the Evil One. Whatever it is, it does not feel good and it does not feel like God. You will do *anything* to keep the old thing from falling apart. This is when you need patience and guidance, and the *freedom to let go* instead of tightening your controls and certitudes. Perhaps Jesus is describing just this phenomenon when he says, "It is a narrow gate and a hard road that leads to life, and only a few find it" (Matthew 7:13-14). Not accidentally, he mentions this narrow road right after teaching the Golden Rule. He knows how much letting go it takes to "treat others as you would like them to treat you" (7:12).

So a change can force a transformation. Spiritual transformation always includes a usually disconcerting reorientation. It can either help people to find a new meaning, or it can force people to close down and turn slowly bitter. The difference is determined precisely by the quality of our inner life, our spirituality. Change just happens, but transformation is always a process of letting go, living in the confusing dark space for awhile, and eventually being spit up on a new and unexpected shore. You can see why Jonah in the belly of the whale is such an important symbol for many Jews and Christians.

In the moments of insecurity and crisis shoulds and oughts don't really help, they just *increase* the shame, guilt, pressure and likelihood of backsliding. It's the deep *yes*es that carry you through. It's that deeper something you are strongly *for* that allows you to wait it out. It's someone you absolutely believe in and your will is committed to. In plain language, love wins out over guilt any day. It is sad that we settle for the short-run effectiveness of shaming people instead of the long-term life benefits of true transformation. But then we are a culture of product and efficiency, not terribly patient with growth. God clearly is much more patient—and finally much more effective. He lets Jonah run in the wrong direction, but finds a long, suffering, circuitous path to get him back where he needs to be—and in spite of himself! That is patient inner transformation. Only God seems to have developed such a talent.

We usually prefer order, control, predictability and "right now." I think that is probably the most striking difference between institutional religion and the God of mercy.

The Loss of Criteria

The previous personal theistic worldview saw things in terms of what was often called "the Great Chain of Being." The great monotheistic religions held God as a clear outer reference point that grounded and originated all things. All lower things were understood in terms of the higher, which gave them an essential importance in the universe. Everything belonged and mirrored the Highest. Within the Great Chain of Being everything is *intrinsically* connected and has *inherent* dignity and meaning: The order was typically: (1) the Divine Realm, (2) the realm of heaven and angels, (3) the human, (4) the animal, (5) the vegetable, (6) the waters and minerals in the earth and (7) the earth itself, which held them all together.

These were all linked in purpose, meaning and sacredness. Our contemporary metaphors for the same are the seamless garment, a cosmic egg (to be examined in Chapter Five), spiritual ecology and the Integrity of all Creation. As long as there is a Transcendent Reference Point, an outer Sacred Source, which communicates Itself, then there is inherent and pervasive meaning in all the other links in the chain. That's an enchanted and coherent universe, inside of which almost all peoples have lived since the beginning of human history. Nothing is profane once you have learned how to see. We are the sad exceptions who live in a dualistic and finally shattered universe, which is no longer a *universe* ("that which turns around one") at all.

Almost all peoples who have lived on the planet were certain about the Highest and therefore moved downward and outward with clarity and noble assurance. This certainty created an objective criterion and reference point for naming the Good, the True and the Beautiful. Thus Saint Francis could even see the divine image in a worm! If there is a creator, everything else is a creature and, in part, reflects the divine image.

Either you see God in Everything or you have lost the basis for seeing God in Anything. Once the dualistic mind takes over, the ego is back into a "pick, choose and decide" game, which is the beginning of exclusionary, punishing and even violent religion. Remember, anthropologically religion begins with the making of a distinction between the pure and the impure. Jesus consistently ignores such a distinction. In fact, it is at the heart of almost half of his gospel actions!

For postmodernism, on the other hand, everything is relative. (That, of course, is ultimately indefensible, because if everything is relative then that principle is relative, too.) Because the contemporary mind has decided that everything is relative instead of relational (a theistic or personalized universe), it forces the individual to manufacture ("make by hand") his or her own greatness. I guess we have confused relative with relational. Relative thinking allows us to dismiss or decrease the energy in everything; relational thinking allows us to increase the energy and kneel in awe before God-in-all-things. I call the first depreciators and the second appreciators.

If God is not the center, *you* are burdened with being the center yourself. What an impossible and self-defeating task. Moment by moment I am at the whim of whimsical desire. "What do *I* want?" or "Am I important now?" become wrong first questions, and keep us trapped in pettiness. Secular people are burdened with finding their own meaning and their private significance. By themselves! It's an impossible and self-defeating task.

Without the inherent dignity that comes from who-you-are-in-God, you will have to become more and more outrageous, more and more bizarre, more and more exaggerated or isolated to make sure that you stand out amid five billion people. The eccentric is the one who lives "outside the center." You expect this of a young person still finding his or her Center, but now many in their 80's still live with such fragile or overpadded egos. You know that we are no longer living in a wisdom culture when even age does not lead to foundation and ground.

Postmodernism ends up with what some call *reductionism.* You can no longer start from the top and find universal meaning reflected through all of creation. Everything is disconnected, standing on its own, unable to validate itself apart from itself. Everything is diminished and demystified. So the best we can normally do is take the lowest level that we can control and understand and move up from there—if we can move up at all. The language of the reductionist often begins with "only" or "just," with suspicion and cynicism. This language will determine ahead of time how much you can see. (The first-rate mind, Ken Wilber, although not a Christian, sees this pattern as the anemic and incomplete eyes of our time. Read almost anything by him if you want to be mightily challenged and moved beyond the reductionist postmodern mind.)

The reductionist and suspicious mind is trapped in a world where it can always be "in charge," which is only at the smallest level and with the most insecure self—your own tiny moment of history, your limited capacity to understand. Nothing great comes from reductionism or suspicious minds, except to initially clear away the bogus issues. Faith instead is the exact opposite: *Faith in its most universal sense is openness to magnanimity, mystery and more.* You do not have to be "religious" to know that is true.

Richard Tarnas's book *The Passion of the Western Mind* helped me to recognize how each century is trapped in its own web, its own limited categories, its own limited way of understanding. Presently, for example, we are trapped in a "market" worldview. This worldview is very pragmatic and very individualistic and its language is the language of romantic expressionism: "I have" and "I choose" are the power statements. Our worldview does not care about greater histories, greater philosophies, greater thinkers or about anything much except the market world of buying and selling. We find ourselves trapped inside of exchange values instead of inherent values, Christians as much as anybody else, very often.

We must be careful that each new revolutionary insight does not return us to our suspicious and deconstructive preferences. I do not disagree, for example, with the feminist critique that we have not heard from women very much in history (or minorities, or gays, or the poor, or the losers of any category, for that matter), but are we really going to say that Aristotle and Erasmus were not gifts to humanity because they happened to be male? Or that Johanna Doe has the truth now because she is a woman? These understandable but knee-jerk reactions to new insights make new ideas more deconstructive than constructive. They only put in place another ten-year period of over-defensiveness and over-compensation. We don't have time for that anymore.

Such either/or deconstruction has unfortunately given academia a very bad name—especially in a country like the United States, which needs all the educated good minds it can get because of its immense worldwide influence. In a certain sense, we had a deconstructionist attitude from the beginnings of the American Revolution, never trusting higher class or culture, or that there might be a good meaning to "nobility." Yet it was some noble-minded men and women who fortunately led us beyond anti-England or anti-anything to a positive and visionary American Project. In general, deconstructionist attitudes are only helpful for initial clarity and focus, but of themselves provide no positive or creative foundation on which to build for the long term.

Gospel Leaven

Postmodernism has tried to overcome the emptiness, or nihilism, of modernism by refusing any worldview to which it will be committed. It could be called a moveable famine, and has no comparable precedent in all of human history. Admittedly modernism's technological scientific explanation of everything did not feed the soul; it was and is empty of deep meaning. So, rather than not be fed, we moved one step further into famine by refusing to be committed to any sustaining food. *Skepticism* is another way to avoid ever having to place your bet, and therefore ever getting hurt. A sort of universal skepticism is a common way of thinking today; critical thinking often looks like intelligence, and sometimes is. You could be a bishop in a church, while totally suspicious and skeptical. Yet you would never be called a heretic! Strange, isn't it?

Skepticism and criticism are fail-safe protection measures for the psyche, but when they dominate, something deep and more important has been abdicated. The human qualities of deference, patience, humility, risk-taking and social grace are also needed for culture and its continuance. Humans grow in such a garden. Jesus does not encourage or expect a world where people are never hurt or never suffer guilt or even injustice. His entire concern is *what we do with mistakes when they happen—always knowing that they will.* "Seventy times seven" is a medicine for a healing community, not for a community with all the answers beforehand and all the appropriate punishments afterwards.

After you've loved and failed a few times, you are afraid to love again. After you have suffered, as the world has in the hundred million killed in war in the twentieth century, you are sure to create some explanations so that you will not have to suffer again. Postmodernism is a way out: no commitments, no surrenders, no absolute anything, no passion for anything—no disappointment, no hurt. On a certain level it makes sense, but after the lessons from the Crucified, we are the people who are being trained in a different way. We do not need to cover all the bases to avoid persecution. In fact, our assumption is that his lifestyle will probably lead to some new forms of persecution.

When we give ourselves to the mystery of Christ, we give ourselves to being hurt, to being on the wheel of life, to walking what we call the way of the cross. No wonder so much of the world resists it! Who wants to be on that wheel? Who wants to enter into solidarity with the tragic mystery of things? Who wants to be formed by the left hand of God? Who wants to bear the dark side? Few I would think: only those who have been led through the mystery of death and resurrection and come out Larger and Awake. (That's probably what the Tradition means by those oft-misunderstood words *chosenness* or *election*.) In that sense, I say Christianity was always intended by Jesus to be a minority position and always will be. *He wasn't dividing the world into those God loved and those God didn't love. Jesus was creating a remnant who were useable by God—to keep the whole world from its violent path toward self-destruction. Jesus is loving and drawing all of us into God.* Or as John put it, "to gather together into one the scattered children of God" (11:52). That is very different than forming a new tribe of saved and superior people.

All I see Jesus talking about is being light, being yeast, being salt and being mustard seed. This is rather prominent both at the beginning of his inaugural address (Matthew 5:13-16) and in his Parabolic Discourse (Luke 13:18-21). It's hard to believe that we missed it in favor of visions of "Christendom," "moral majorities," managerial institutions, electorates and "your excellencies." It kept us in the imperial ego-mind, as opposed to the surrendered, trusting mind of Jesus. It seems that, in earthly terms, all Jesus ever intended was a yeast of truth that would be a change agent or preservative in history. Ironically, it looked much more like an immoral minority than any moral majority! His plan was truly subversive, and is the only one that ever has a chance of true victory. As someone once said, "Conservatives are just those who are enamored with present evils, while liberals want to replace present evils with new ones." The gospel is beyond this whole mindset.

The story line haunts us all, and still disappoints pretenders to power on left or right. The Jesus story stands as a revelatory judgment on every other story line, trial and legal system in the world. It is still a shock and even a bit of a disappointment: *Jesus has a lot of hope in sinners* (which is good news for just about everybody, and why they called it so). *Jesus only has problems with those who don't think they are sinners.* This turns all religious history upside down. The search for so-called purity is over. Now the only issue is honesty and humility. We call it by the hard word *repentance.*

In any human scenario, even when we don't want to believe it, we know that the characters are at least and always three: Jesus, the bad guys and the supposed good guys. What Jesus says is: Be prepared to be surprised about who is who. This leaven of the gospel is inexorably chipping away at such things as capital punishment, wars against the poor, war rationales in general, legal systems, idealizations of the wealthy and those at the top, traditions of human torture and oppression, and something as recent as the inability of the American Congress, despite its best attempts, to unseat a "sinful" president! That would never have happened except in a culture that is gospel-trained in empathy for the victim. Once many perceived that the president was becoming the victim, they changed to his side!

The gospel story line will have the final chapter of history. God is winning. And it is good news for *all* the people, especially for those who don't yet know they are also "under the mercy." Again and again it creates an ability for humanity to "pull down the mighty from their thrones and lift up the lowly" (Luke 1:52). It is no accident that these revolutionary words come from Mary, the feminine and first believer in Jesus.

Man-Movement-Machine-Monument-Memory

They say that all great things in history start with an individual person. For the sake of alliteration and memory we will say "man." If that person has something to say that is alive and real and names reality correctly it often moves to the second stage of a "movement." That's the period of the greatest energy. The Church, for example, is at its greatest vitality as "the God Movement," and the institution is merely the vehicle for that movement. Neither pope nor president can ever control the movement itself, by any theology, doctrine or dogma. We cannot control the blowing of the Spirit. It is to the mature credit of the Roman Church that it was able to teach this officially at the time of Vatican Council II. (See especially the documents on the Church and the decree on non-Christian religions.) The Movement stage is always very exciting, creative—and also risky.

It's risky because the movement of God in history is larger than any denomination, any culture, any tradition's ability to verbalize it. We feel out of control here, and yet why would anybody want it to be anything less than that? Do we really want to think that the great God could be in our little pockets? Would we respect a God that we could control? Would we really respect a Church who presumed it could predict and contain God's actions? I don't think so, yet that is what so much immature religion seems to want—control over God by worshiping God "correctly." Thus we move rather quickly out and beyond the dangerous movement stage to the machine stage. This is predictable and understandable, even if unfortunate.

The institutional or "machine" stage of a Movement will necessarily be *a less alive manifestation*, which is not bad, although always surprising for those who see Church as an end in itself instead of merely a vehicle for the vision. But, we need "the less noble" parts of the Body to keep us all growing toward love (1 Corinthians 12:22-24). We can also learn from the less mature stages of life. The steps to maturity, in fact, are always steps through immaturity. There is no other way. But when we do not realize the limited capacities of a machine, we try to make it into something more than it is. We make it a monument, a closed system operating inside of its own, often self-serving, logic.

It's the nature of the beast and a seemingly inevitable movement, especially as we get tied up with job security, consistent policies for everything and public image and identity. As soon as you get employment norms and professional people whose job depends on status, security and dependability, it's very hard to take risks for God or for the values of the gospel. Eventually this monument, its maintenance and self-preservation become ends in themselves. Jeremiah rails against such formalization at the beginnings of his prophecy: Put no trust in delusive words like, the temple, the temple, the temple! While you follow alien gods....."I am not blind—it is Yahweh who speaks" (see 7:11). Monuments need to be regularly deconstructed and rebuilt. Thus Thomas Jefferson told the first American revolutionaries that this revolution had to be repeated in some form every twenty-five years!

Truth is never actualized until it becomes my truth, suffered for, owned and internalized. Surely authentic religion can settle for nothing less. Let me use here a clarifying and dense quote from John Stuart Mill (from *On Liberty*). He is warning us against the monument and machine stages:

> Even if the received opinion be not only true, but the whole truth; unless it is suffered to be, and actually is, vigorously and earnestly contested, it will, by most of those who receive it, *be held in the manner of a prejudice*, with little comprehension or feeling of its rational grounds.

Each generation has to appropriate its deepest beliefs for itself. We used to say it this way, "God has no grandchildren"! Each generation must itself be realigned with God, and discover the mystery for itself. Yet we want the results of someone else's homework. A machine become monument is now in place. It is so easy to just step on board, without ever knowing why or feeling the longing ourselves. The man and movement stages have been entirely jumped over, and we have "God's frozen people" instead of any hint of chosen, beloved or journey status. In this state religion is merely an excuse to remain unconscious, a "memory" of something that must once have been a great adventure. Now religion is no longer life itself, but actually a substitute for life, or worse, an avoidance of life. But God has no grandchildren; only children. The secret is to know how to keep in touch with the man and movement stages, without being naive about the necessity of some machine, and the inevitability of those who love monuments. And we must be honest. All of us love monuments when they are monuments to *our* man, our movement, or our machine.

Ordinary People

Sometimes machine and monument folks can be recaptured by the vision of the man and movement. At the Center for Action and Contemplation in Albuquerque, we were often visited by our friend Frank Strabala (who died in 1999). He worked for the nuclear test site outside of Las Vegas, Nevada. In fact Frank was the head of it for a number of years—and then dared by the grace of the gospel to call it into question. He even joined me once as we practiced civil disobedience at the test site. I will never forget his walking toward me with a half-worried, half-smile on his face. "I have trusted your teaching all these years, now I have to trust where it has led me," he said. We stood together as his former employees drove by and gave a less than flattering gesture to their old boss. I was humbled and awed by such courage and such humility. He had exchanged his secure monument through an encounter with the man Jesus, and the vision of the peace movement.

It's hard and very rare to call your own job into question. When Jesus called his disciples, he also called them away from their jobs and their families! (See for example, Matthew 4:22.) Now those don't sound like bad things, do they? He called them to leave their nets because as long as you are tied to job security, there are a lot of things you cannot see and you cannot say. This is one of the great recurring disadvantages of clergy earning their salary from the Church, and perhaps why Francis did not want us to be ordained priests! You tend to think and say whatever won't undermine the company store.

Anyone who has ever worked for another understands this, and I wonder if it is not at the bottom of so much anti-clericalism among the blue-collar workers of the world. They often see right through our clergy pretensions. As one smart construction worker once angrily said to me, "Would you really bother to try to prove or defend papal infallibility or who can 'transubstantiate' if you did not have a vested interest in the answer? Those are the prefab answers of people in management, but they are not even the questions of those in labor!" Wow. We must be humble enough to hear. I know he has a point when I see the glazed eyes of the parents in the front pew as we sermonize about the glories of Holy Orders and celibacy!

Jesus called the disciples away from their natural family, too. If there's another blindness that keeps you from bigger truth—and it's an even more sacred cow than job—it is family. Families are either very good or very bad for human growth, but in either case they are only runways for takeoff. As others have said, family provides roots, but the wings have to come from elsewhere.

What if we went home tonight, gathered the kids in a circle and said, "We are getting rid of the TV." That would be very hard to do without a larger support system. Those kinds of wings to a larger world seldom can be grown inside of the nuclear family. All we can do is give the love and security foundation so that they can ask such daring questions later, but they usually cannot come from home. In fact, family holds many people behind a very safe and often small "white picket fence." It is not even roots for many people, much less wings, only a brick wall to hit against or to be encircled by.

That's why Jesus insists on asking bigger questions than the immediate family usually can. Jesus tells us, don't get too secure in your job and don't assume that your small family has all the answers. This seems to be an Eastern wisdom that is more common in Asiatic cultures. The small family is very tight, but also tightly ensconced inside of extended family, neighborhood, religion and traditions. Sadly we have neither!

In India, for example, a man cannot get on to the third and last stages of full life until he has left the second. The four stages are: student, householder, forest dweller/seeker and finally wise man. In the practical West, we stop at stage two, and increasingly do not have the skills for even doing that stage well. I am sure this is part of the explanation of why our wisdom is so small, as is our insular politics, and our tribal view of so much of the Church.

Most of our men have not made many journeys away from "Mama"—and maternal Churches and companies (see my books, *The Wild Man's Journey* [St. Anthony Messenger Press, 1996] and *Quest for the Grail* [Crossroad, 1994]). Because their male journey has not been spiritually negotiated, many spend the rest of their lives trying to marry Mama (ask many wives), afraid of any real intimacy with women or needing the security systems that Mama always provides.

As a priest of thirty years, I am continually struck by how many of our most fervent Catholic men (including priests) are also very soft and security-conscious men, not risk-takers in any sense. Mama Church and Mother Mary dressed in blue are preferred to the Sermon on the Mount or 40 days in *any* desert. This has profoundly affected the very character of the gospel that has been preached. We have not yet left home, so the gospel itself is highly domesticated.

When the safe assumptions of society and family reach the monument stage, you might think you need TNT or major surgery to break through. But you never win with any frontal attack on the mystery of evil. You only become a mirror image of it, but better disguised. Jesus calls that trying to drive out the devil by the prince of devils (see Luke 11:14-22).

So instead, Francis of Assisi went out to the edge and did it better. If you attack something directly, you let it determine the energy, the style, the opposition. You soon become the same thing, but in a disguised and denied form. That's how evil expands so successfully. The disguise is almost perfect, and without spiritual discernment, will fool the best of us. So Francis respects the monuments, even loves them, but also goes back to the original dynamism and nonviolent style of Jesus the man for his inspiration.

If you have been to Assisi, there are the walls and inside them there are the cathedral and the established churches, all of which are fine. That's where Francis first heard the gospel and fell in love with Jesus. But then he quietly goes outside the walls and rebuilds some old ruins called San Damiano and the Portiuncula. He's not with his mouth telling the others they're doing it wrong, he just gently, lovingly tries to do it better. I think that's true reconstruction. Remember, *the best criticism of the bad is the practice of the better*. That might be a perfect motto for all reconstructive work. It does not destroy machines or even monuments, but reinvigorates them with new energy and form. San Damiano was still a church building, but it was small, poor and on the edge.

Moral Realism

There is a book called *The Ignorant Perfection of Ordinary People* (State University of New York Press, 1991). The brilliant title says it all. In it, Robert Inchausti speaks of the spiritual longings of ordinary people as the basis for most great social and political reforms. He calls it so rightly "Constructive Postmodernism"! This is exactly what we are talking about here: people who know the dark side, but build anyway. Not naive denial, not Pollyanna idealism, not utopianism, but the true biblical *hope that is received only on the other side of suffering and failure*. Most of us either become paralyzed or think we are enlightened because we know about the problems, the sin, the scandal, the essentially tragic nature of human existence. We go through the deconstructive stage without the reconstructive gift of vision and hope. That's probably the main burden of being a non-believer or a mere ideologue: the forlorn or cynical attitude of so many academics and social activists.

I meet people of "ignorant perfection" every now and then, and I am always in awe at God's subtle work of art in them. It is like meeting an unselfconscious but strikingly beautiful man or woman. These folks are usually traditional in their values. Maybe they still appear to be "first naiveté" people. They're usually very commonsense. There's a moral realism in healthy and grounded people. They're not ideological on the left or the right. They can accept people whom others have judged for one reason or another. They don't move up in their head and form great big explanations for why it's wrong or why it's right. You can never shock them. They do not read reality first of all with their moral compass, but with the eyes of compassion. They don't bring answers down from above, but find them within and evoke them from below. And for some reason: They don't compare! They take what is right in front of them on its own self-evident terms, giving each person the benefit of the doubt.

I think I love and look for people like this because my father, Richard Rohr (1910-1999), Kansas farmer and railroad worker, was that kind of man. I have also met simple nuns who work with prostitutes and orderlies at the jail, who deal patiently with whatever is right in front of them, not even thinking to call it patience. Somehow they have been rebuilt in a new form. My assumption is that once they were "unbuilt," stripped down to the core, and learned how to live from that clear and humbled point.

This moral realism is not a moral skepticism or abdication, but ironically a true and enlightened traditionalism. Only the shape of human sin changes in each age, but we are always pointing to the same illusions and false promises of the ego (thus, the perennial truth of ancient typologies like the Enneagram, and the capital sins or "demons" of most traditions). The patterns that each generation must maneuver are the same as our ancestors, and someone who has once touched the face and name of sin in themselves is never shocked again. Evil, like God, is One, which is probably why we personified it in Satan. But once you smell the scent of Satan, it shows up in all kinds of shapes and forms, none of which surprise you anymore. They only sharpen you.

What has made this sharpening difficult is that all information (not wisdom) since the beginning of time has increased exponentially in the last generation. We are always expecting the final and truthful answer to show itself. This explosion of data makes us think that wisdom is still out in front of us. Unfortunately, we turn away from the pregnant "now," from our ancestors, from the healing power of memory. We reject healthy traditionalism, even transformative traditionalism, in favor of a future answer that is never quite there. Because when it comes, it is soon a rejected "old" idea, too—and another guru is on the scene within two months. Just watch the flow of self-help books and how quickly their fleeting fame passes.

By very traditional wisdom or moral realism I refer to qualities or states of being such as silence, solitude, detachment, honesty, confession, forgiveness, radical humility. No new author or book is going to do better than these. We hope they will just help us understand them better. And there is nothing very spectacular about any of these disciplines— no dependence on crystals, prophecies, auspicious days or highly trained priest class. Ordinary people discover this wisdom by *living!*

Probably the single most traditional wisdom issue is, of course, the immense teaching capacity of human suffering, and especially unjust suffering. Probably none of the world religions deal with it in a more up-front and utterly dramatic way than Christianity. We are, after all, the only religion that worships the victim. As discussed earlier in this book, we proclaimed the scapegoated one to be the very "Lord of History." It seems that God must be trying to answer a very central human problem in coming among us as a Crucified and Forgiving Victim. I ask again, isn't this—sooner or later—at the heart of everybody's spiritual problem: what we do with our pain?

Why evil? Why suffering? Even Job can't get an answer, and Job, I think, is the epitome of moral development in the Hebrew Scriptures. He is the same story as Jesus. Job begs for the answer, and finally trusts when he knows that God is taking him seriously and he is simply "in the conversation" (see Job 42). Jesus later *becomes* the answer in his passion, death and resurrection. But it is really the same answer: God can be trusted. The world is still safe, coherent and even blessed. We are saved by being addressed and included in a cosmic conversation. We do not really need answers; we only need to be taken seriously as part of the dialogue. But we only know this in hindsight after the suffering and the struggle. It cannot be known theoretically or theologically or before the fact. That is the big rub, the perennial disappointment. I cannot copy from someone else's homework. I can only be inspired by them, and that is a good start.

Our knowledge of God is participatory. God refuses to be intellectually "thought," and is only known in the passion and pain of it all, when the issues become soul-sized and worthy of us. One of the lay women mystics is supposed to have asked Jesus in one of her locutions,

"Why, Jesus, is there so much pain on the earth? Why do people have to suffer?" And Jesus said back to her, "Catherine, if there were any other way I would have thought of it a long time ago" (Saint Catherine of Genoa, *The Spiritual Dialogue*). There's no other way we learn how to let go and to learn compassion it seems. There is no other way that we will give up control until we are led to the limits of our own resources—and must rely upon another. Then we know the Ground of our Being. Don't trust any spiritual teacher who has not suffered. And don't look for any teacher who predicts the future, only one who can lead you to peace with the past and, especially, with the sufferings of the past.

CHAPTER FIVE

The Cosmic Egg of Meaning

· · · · · · · · · · · · · · · · ·

IF WE ARE GOING to be the rebuilders of society, we need to be "rebuilt" ourselves. A healthy psyche lives within at least three containers of meaning. Let me explain. Imagine three domes or levels of meaning. The first is called "My Story," the second is "Our Story" and the third is "*The* Story." This is what I call the cosmic egg. It is the unique and almost unconscious gift of all healthy religion. Much of the genius of the biblical revelation is that it honors and integrates all three. Much of the weakness of deconstructed society is that it usually honors only one level at best, and thus treats that level very poorly. Most postmodern people are trapped inside the smallest container if they are secular individualists, the second container if they are merely cultural conservatives, and they are trapped in a false version of the third if they are fundamentalist in any form. The saint/whole/healed person lives happily inside of all three.

I. This Is Me (My Story)

The modern, and now postmodern world, is the first period of history where a large number of people have been allowed to take their private lives and identities seriously. Many of our parents did not even have a language for it. There is a wonderful movement into individuation here, but there is also a diminishment and fragility if that is all we have. (*Individuation*, by the way, is a positive word to describe an appropriate sense of self, ego and boundaries. Individualism, however, refers to the exaggerated sense of self, ego and overprotected boundaries.)

In this first dome is my private life, those issues that make me special, inferior, superior, right, wrong, handicapped or gifted, depending on how "I" see it. "I" and its feelings and opinions are the reference

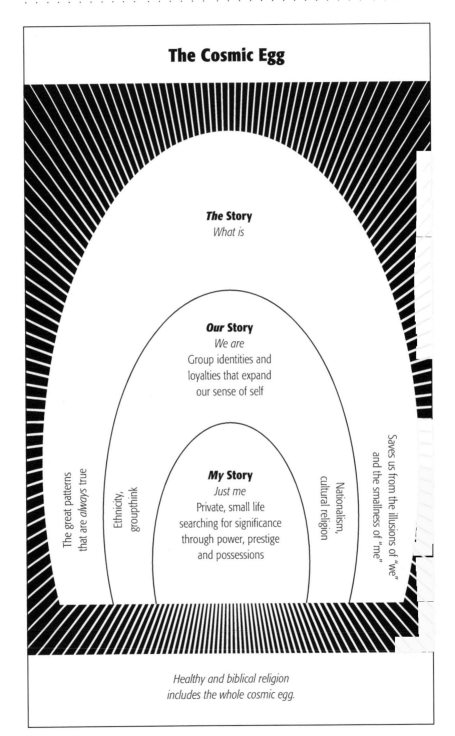

The Cosmic Egg

The Story
What is

Our Story
We are
Group identities and
loyalties that expand
our sense of self

My Story
Just me
Private, small life
searching for significance
through power, prestige
and possessions

The great patterns
that are *always* true

Ethnicity,
groupthink

Nationalism,
cultural religion

Saves us from the illusions of " we"
and the smallness of " me"

*Healthy and biblical religion
includes the whole cosmic egg.*

point for everything. This is exactly what you must let go of in early prayer practice, and yet this is the very tiny and false self that contemporary people take as normative and even sufficient.

The dome of "This Is Me" is about all the postmodern person has left: my power, my prestige and my possessions. It's the little stage where you do *your* dance and where the questions are usually "Who is watching me? How do *I* feel? What do *I* believe? What makes me unique?" It's a passing arena, to be certain. It will be over in a few years, and is frankly boring if it is all you have to talk about. My Story is not big enough or true enough to create large or meaningful patterns by itself.

But many people live their whole lives at this level of anecdote and nurtured self-image, without ever connecting with the larger domes of meaning. They *are* what they have done and what has been done to them. Nothing more. You can see how fragile and unprotected, and therefore, constantly striving this self will be. It is very easily offended, fearful and therefore often posturing and pretentious.

My opinion is that if we stay in this smallest dome of meaning, we often move toward a neurotic self-image. Jean Houston put it in her own language when she said, "When we do not have mythology, all we have left is pathology." This small and fragile self needs to be a part of something more significant—and so it creates dramas, tragedies and victimhoods to put itself on a larger stage. Just watch American television, where trivia and drivel is raised to an art form—as much by the evening news, political commentators and religious programming as by the easily criticized talk shows. Unfortunately that's the primary paradigm we live out of today: merely episodic meaning bolstering up the tiny and disconnected self. A woman claims to be receiving apparitions from Mary, a gunman wants to get his picture in the paper: Both are isolating and episodic, but trying to be cosmic.

I recently saw a cartoon that depicted a pair of restroom doors. Instead of one bathroom saying male and one saying female, the one said "evil oppressors" and the other bathroom said "victims." What a simplistic and, finally, destructive way to image reality, yet that is our recent politically correct framework. It gives the small self a sense of being a part of some national drama, as we constantly decide who is which, who is bad and who is the hero. Life as a giant whodunit seems to be the secular form of heaven and hell.

The small self is intrinsically unhappy, because it has no ontological foundation. It is not real. It does not exist. It will always be insecure, afraid and scrambling for significance. The purely secular project is doomed to creating catastrophe. The stage isn't big enough for us all to be special on this little earth—except under the sacred canopy of the larger domes of meaning. In Jesus' language, "the branch cut off from the Vine is useless" (John 15:5).

II. This Is Us (Our Story)

The next and larger realm of meaning is about "Us." This is the dome of our group, our community, our country, our Church—perhaps our nationality or ethnic group. For young people it is often their friends, their gang or even their kind of music. We seem to need this to contain our own identity and security as social beings. Again, it is both good and necessary. If you do not have a group or, at least, family that you can bond with, you create an asocial being, a sociopath or a psychopath incapable of bonding anywhere. Most of us have multiple member-ships: family, neighborhood, church, country. These are our schools for relationship, connection and almost all virtue as we know it.

Everyone has this level of meaning, consciously or unconsciously, negatively or positively. If you don't, you are autistic. We are essential-ly social beings and we live inside of some shared meanings, which become our reference points, our runway. It is the necessary training ground for belonging, attaching, trusting and loving. If you bond in a healthy family, know that your race is somehow "chosen," are proud of your religion and your group possibilities—you might just write the Bible! Some folks unfortunately just spend their lives defending the boundaries and "glory" of their group. They write programs for war, scapegoating and major illusion, or at least for smallness. Only group egocentricity is more dangerous than personal egocentricity. It looks like greatness when it is often no more than disguised egotism.

The second dome of meaning gives you myth, cultural heroes, group symbols, flags, special foods, ethnicity and patriotism. These tell you that you are not alone; you are also connected to a larger story. We all know that it is fanciful, but it is *shared* meaning and that is impor-tant. That we all know the same story of George Washington cutting down the cherry tree is more important than its actually being true. But a lot of people stop at the level of shared meaning because it gives a lot more consolation and a lot more security to the small self. In fact, the loyalties at this level have driven most of human history up to now.

These identities run so deep that many people have died and given their lives for their group, their country, their religious group. It is one step removed from True Transcendence, so it often becomes an easy substitute for God. Watch people and their emotions in regard to war, flag, religion, team. To die for these feels like dying for God, and that is why it takes so little to talk young men, for example, into dying in war.

Men seem especially prone to the consolations of group belonging, perhaps because they are less good at personal intimacy. Women will die for a child; men prefer to die for a cause. Clearly we are dealing with archetypal meanings here. If you have not contacted the third level, these are your only gods.

People try to find identity in a group, in an institutional affiliation, in a nation, in a public cause, or today like never before, in public fame or infamy. Somehow to be on the news and in the papers is to be "immortalized." It takes away much of the anxiety of developing a personal self. You feel protected inside of the group identity or public fame. We all get into being one ethnic group or another, Catholic, a Harley-Davidson bike owner, a Chicago Cubs fan, and then sport proud signs about it! It lifts some real burden from our private striving, and there is true comfort in being among your own. Now you don't have to be great by yourself, you can ride on the coattails of other Polish Americans and other owners of golden retrievers!

A lot of Americans bought the second level especially after the World Wars of this century. It became the operative mythology of this country. How fine to think of the glory of being American; we were the liberators of Europe and the good guys in almost every conceivable context! This romanticized mythology served us very well (not, however, the rest of the world), until it began to unravel in the 1960's with the Vietnam War, the Civil Rights Movement, the assassinations and the hippie movement's wholesale cultural rejection of the cultural illusions.

Although deconstruction began in Europe much earlier, it did not really happen in America until the 1960's, and some would date it precisely at 1968. Things are definitely different before and after 1968, and we are still in the process of trying to understand what fell apart and why. It felt so good before it must have been right, some think. (American Catholics suffer it on two levels with the Second Vatican Council ending at about the same time. Thus there is the terrible temptation to idealize something that once was, but was also a mixed blessing, just as the now is.)

The great "This Is Us" dome is summed up in that common phrase, "For God and Country." It was engraved above so many lintels, the motto of so many organizations and at the top of so many letterheads in America, that most Christians never stopped to realize that it was both heresy and idolatry! And, of course, each group had God all to themselves, just the way our Jewish ancestors wanted to keep God in their Temple, while still daring to call Yahweh "the Lord of heaven and earth." Tribal gods tend to flourish in second-dome people.

After teaching and observing Churches in all continents, I am still amazed that Americans are not bothered by the flag in the sanctuary of our "catholic" churches. I am also amazed that God tends to look like a banker in Switzerland, a reserved gentleman in England and a crucified but not resurrected Jesus in fatalistic cultures. But you can't see what you can't see, I guess. Groupthink assures a rather total form of blindness. Most women themselves did not consciously recognize the evils of sexism and patriarchy until the 1980's.

In all my growing up in Kansas I can honestly say I never heard in our Catholic Church any anti-Protestant sermons or sentiments. We never put them down, we just felt sorry for them! Sorry, but we did! We, like all groups, were comfortable inside our own self-assured universe. Their churches were so ugly, we thought. Why would anyone want to go to those churches, when ours are full of gold, statues, pictures, incense, candles and color! Our churches were brimming with meaning! All those stories of saints and miracles! We had apparitions on a regular basis. Mary only appeared to us and never to them. Ours was a totally enchanting world. Theirs was sort of sad and desperate. (Some new young Catholics are thinking this way again, unfortunately.)

We never realized, of course, that other children were growing up in their traditions, loving their own worlds just as much as we loved ours—and fearing ours in comparison. Notice all of the "us" and "them" language in the above paragraph. That is the way the mind works when it lives primarily under the second dome. It is good and necessary, but finally illusory and dangerous to pitch camp there.

Catholicism, Americanism, Masonic Lodges, any subculture or mythic system, works like a good joke: You either get it or you don't. If you don't get it, you don't get it. If you *do* get it, you tend to be subsumed beneath its spell—for good or for ill. It becomes a nonrational frame of reference that is hard to shake. I will meet Ph.D.'s who will come to me with the most infantile sense of God or of evil, but you know it is their childhood myth still guiding their lives. You normally can't change this childhood myth totally later in life, and will usually revert to it in times of crisis or chaos. On the positive side, if we are raised with wonderful mythic stories, which formed us at a deep, archetypal level, we will also return there for sanity and solace. They will be safe containers for the rest of our lives.

The pre-Vatican II "Catholic story" gave you a strong sense of We Are. It was a rather watertight system, as long as it remained isolated and self-assured. This is true today of groups like the Amish and the Mormons and the Catholic gathering in St. Mary's, Kansas. It is much easier to do if you remain autonomous and separate, which is why the entire Law of Holiness (see Leviticus 11-26) and most of the books of Leviticus and Numbers are about *how to be separate*. Many people never move beyond this early stage because it gives so much identity and comfort—even though it lacks breadth, depth and compassion. For many people, like early Judaism, separation and holiness are almost identical terms! Jesus, of course, rejects the Law of Holiness in favor of the Law of Universal Compassion. That's a *much* more difficult path: integration rather than separation and segregation.

You must have "commitment-fostering mechanisms" to maintain life at the second level: symbols, songs, sacred times, places and, especially, sacrificial things that you all agree to. There is no strong sense of being together in life unless you *do* some things together, especially it seems, things that are strange, visible and demand constant sacrificial choice. Wearing black veils almost defines some Arab womanhood—and it works. Not eating meat on Friday probably made little difference to God, but it sure held us together. All bowing toward Mecca at the same time is a magnificent cultural practice.

It really works very well, but the trouble is that it feels so godly that *much, if not most, religion is a belonging system more than a search for intimacy with God*. The trouble is that the "Founder of our Firm," Jesus, emphasized none of these! He was not into tribal religion, groupthink and loyalty tests. Much of the institutional Church is, however, and always has been. It works too well to call it into question. It holds us together, and that feels like salvation, even if it is a very deteriorated form of it.

God could care less, I'm convinced, but God seems to know that *we* need it. *We* need it so the soul can be settled and trustful, *we* need it to get started, *we* need it for communal encouragement and support. When we knew that *all of us* were eating our fish on Friday, that gave us a great sense of group loyalty and sacrifice for a common cause. It gave us a sense of "the heroic" that religion seems to call for.

The common experience, however, is that you will need it less and less as you move toward the Real Center. Thus you often see a certain freedom in kind old folks, Jubilarian religious and people who have suffered. In the second half of life, you don't need to be a hero anymore, just *real*. Augustine put it most daringly: "Love God and do what you will"!

The more demanding this communal act is, the better it works. The only religions that are growing today are those that ask a lot from their people. The more liberal they are, the more they're falling apart. Young Hispanic men in New Mexico are attracted to "no drink, no sex, no gambling" religion much more than our calm, contemplative and friendly Catholicism. This is a real problem, because I do believe the second is much more mature and closer to the spirit of Jesus, but we need to understand why Jesus religion normally has to be preceded by John the Baptist religion.

In more ways than we thought, John is the "precursor" of Jesus. (I try to address this in *The Wild Man's Journey* in an attempt to understand the Promise Keepers Movement and the "heroic" needs of the young male.) It seems we normally begin "conservative" (with structure, order, certitude, absolutes that must eventually fail us!), and we move toward more tolerant, risk-taking, exception-granting behavior. Again, you must know the rules before you can "break" the rules or know what the rules really mean. It is great to start with John the Baptist but end with Jesus. "No man born of woman is greater than John, but the least born into the reign of God is better than he" (Matthew 11:11).

III. The Patterns That Are Always True (Universal Meaning)

Now let's move to the third and largest dome of meaning, what Peter Berger would call "The Sacred Canopy." This is the realm of universal meaning, *The* Story that is always true, the Patterns that every culture and religion discover in some manner. This level assures and insures the other two, it holds them together in sacred meaning. This is True Transcendence, authentic Spirit which informs all soul and body work. This is what secularism has rejected. Postmodernism says *there are no* "universal narratives" that are always true. The cosmic egg is then cracked because the greatest container is rejected—"and all the king's horses and all the king's men" do not seem capable of putting it back together again. The cosmic egg is uniquely the work of God and healthy religion.

Biblical religion, at its best, honors and combines all three levels: personal journey as raw material, communal identity as school and training ground, True Transcendence as the integration and gathering place for all the parts together. We call it holiness, which is the ultimate form of wholeness. The three great monotheistic religions of Judaism,

Islam and Christianity also make this third level personal. This meaning is not just an idea but a Person.

Without the Great Stories that free us from the tyranny and the idolatry of the first two stories, we remain trapped in small cultural and private worlds. Without the Great Patterns that are always true, we get lost in choosing between tiny patterns. True Transcendence frees us from the tyranny of the I Am and the idolatry of the We Are. But if all three are taken seriously, as the Bible does very well, we have a full life—fully human and fully divine.

Some, perhaps more foolish than all, try to fly like Icarus to the Great Story, without the fumbling and constant humiliations of My Story and Our Story. That's fundamentalism. It looks like passionate religion, but it is not Incarnation, it is not biblical, it is not wisdom. It emerged largely in the last century when we forgot how to read sacred literature and were trapped in very limited notions of how to express truth. Ironically, it seems to indicate a kind of dumbing down of human consciousness, a kind of limiting of meaning so that we can understand it, control it and always be able to explain it.

Liberal types—well-educated, therapeutic, psychological people—tend to get trapped today in the first dome of private meaning and their educated explanations. Thus, they are very prone to individualistic worldviews—my ability to choose, my consciousness and my freedom are what make an action good, not whether it is really good for society or for the other.

Conservatives tend to get trapped in the second dome of group and tribal loyalties. They desire some kind of common worldview, but then they stop there. Everything is waving the flag of America or the papacy or the Bible or the NRA. In some circles today, you would think we were worshiping the pope instead of Jesus! (It does hold the group together in a time when there is little loyalty to anything. Remember how Yahweh gave in to the Jewish demand for a king, even though he said that they were rejecting him in this request [see 1 Samuel 8].)

But both progressive thinking and traditional thinking can be a way to avoid the great surrender to God. They have much more to do with personal temperament or needs for control than with any classical spiritual path. To both of them, *the act of faith will still feel like dying* (to their own constructs and certitudes). And both will find their own excuses to explain away why they should have to "die"—exactly what Jesus did not do.

The person who lives within the total cosmic egg is the mystic, the prophet, the universal man or woman, the saint, the whole one. These are people like Mahatma Gandhi, Saint Bonaventure, Martin Luther King, Mother Teresa, Cardinal Newman, Dag Hammerskjöld and Julian of Norwich (my favorite mystic); these are the people who look out—with eyes wide as saucers—at the smaller pictures because they observe from the utterly big picture. These are the ones who can both honor and listen to the little stories and also live in the final state of affairs already now. They are often called seers because their perspective contains all the eyes, even somehow the eyes of God.

The Great Ones are beyond mere group loyalties, beyond any simple dualistic thinking that always puts them on the right side, beyond winners and losers, good guys and bad guys. Lawrence Kohlberg would probably call them Stage Six People, who live by universal principles, while still caring for the specific; honoring cultural norms, yet making room for the exceptions. They have seen in a contemplative way, beyond the shadow and the disguise, beyond the suffocating skin of the private self and the self-serving egotisms of group. Aldous Huxley calls this mystical knowing the "perennial philosophy." It is the contemplative mind that integrates and gives focus to all our calculating and controlling. Without it, there is only civil and self-serving religion.

However we are going to reconstruct, it's going to come from people who can see in this way. *True reconstruction will be led by those who can see reality at all three levels simultaneously.* They can honor the Divine level and live ultimately inside of a Great Big Story Line. They will appreciate the needs and context of the Group Story and not dismiss it as mere culture trappings or meaningless traditions. They won't say that the Small Story is not important either. They won't demean or dismiss people who are working on personal issues or facing the important identity issues of the first half of life.

And most importantly, don't think you can separate one from the other. It is not sequential, but simultaneous. Many in our therapeutic society think they first must get it together personally and then they will serve groups or search for God. It all happens in a spiral, it seems to me, and, in fact, there is a natural ecology of checks and balances between the three domes of meaning. I, like many of you who grew up before deconstruction, was lucky and blessed enough to have good family, good religion and community, and good therapy and time for self-knowledge—overlapping one another like waves from an endless sea. Most people emphasize only one or the other. Think about that, and you will have to agree. It is like a major work of art to discover someone today who honors all three levels.

The Need for Boundaries and Limits

Boundaries seem to be the only way that human beings can find a place to stand, a place to begin, a place to move out from. Even those who think they don't have any usually do. You know it when you trespass against them. Howard Thurman, the venerable black mystic, said, "Just be careful before you move anybody else's boundary markers." The human soul has to have face and ground, especially in the first years of life. You can't *begin* liberal, you must begin with some boundaries, some givens, some criteria and even absolutes, if nothing else than to give you a "goad to kick against" (Acts 26:14).

As Paul belabors in his letter to the Romans, *the Law is given for the sake of information, education, and transformation* (see especially chapters 2-7), but is not itself "enlightenment." Even though allegiance to boundaries, limits and laws is almost universally confused with religion and even salvation itself, "the law will not save anyone" (Galatians 3:11). It has to do with the pattern of how transformation happens, that's all. The struggle with boundaries and law creates the wrestling ring, but is not itself the encounter nor the victory.

Human beings seem to need to fight and engage with something before they can take it seriously—and before they can discover what they really need and what they really want. *The people who never fight religion, guilt, parents, injustice, friends, marriage partners and laws usually have no deep and free "respect" for their power and importance.* That is probably why you have to begin conservative in a certain sense. Any good therapist knows that this is true, as does any cultural anthropologist. The spoiled child, the soft culture, the entitled adult never produce very much.

It's amazing to me how many creative people had parental or religious goads that they are still kicking against! In fact, it is almost the norm. Adam and Eve, Jacob, Job, Paul and the Magdalene would be scriptural examples. Jesus put it very cleverly, drawing on Psalm 118: The stone which the builders *reject* is, in fact, the keystone (see Psalm 118:22; Matthew 21:42). Much of the best teaching in the Church has emerged precisely in response to condemnations, denials, refusals, rejections, failures and sin. If you want the best minds in the world to work on an idea, just have Rome condemn it or Washington forbid it. Many of the great saints had at least one difficult parent, like Francis himself. Limits and edges seem to refine things. Shapelessness is just that.

Søren Kierkegaard, the Danish philosopher and theologian, said that the "aesthetic person" and the "moral person" were the most common disguises and avoidances for the truly religious person. True religion, according to Kierkegaard, is about the one who makes that scary "leap of faith" where he gives up all control and trust to One he loves, and not just one who safely buries his credits for later redemption (see Luke 19:11-27). Cult and code feel religious, but they are only the window dressing.

If we are looking for directions for reconstruction, I think we can usually look at *the human need* that conservatives are trying to name. *The way* they are saying it is usually too righteous and angry *the rigid solutions* they offer are often elitist, protective of power and the past but *the need* that they are usually pointing toward is legitimate in some form. People do need some degree of order, predictability, security and authority *to begin* to function well. You need to be John the Baptist before you can be Jesus, normally. The trouble is that most Christians are, in fact, followers of John the Baptist, who is only good as far as he goes. I had that structure for most of my life, and I still do—which is exactly why I don't need it! It is now, at least in part, internalized and operative.

I admit that conservatives are often clinging to their positions with an anger and reaction that seems unwarranted. They're usually appealing to worst-case scenarios, overreacting to their loss of control and often fall into group loyalty as a substitute for biblical faith. But give them this much credit: They're saying that human beings need some absolute criteria, some reference points, some givens; we cannot live in constant flux and re-discernment of everything. They are just asking for the Sacred Canopy!

The psyche cannot live with everything changing everyday, everything a matter of opinion, everything relative. You can't build any great civilization when everything is up for grabs. There must be a sound container holding you long enough so you can move beyond survival mode. Most people move into siege mentality and never find time for creativity. Yet with the information explosion of this century, many people are moving into greater instability and anxiety, even neurosis.

That probably explains why John Paul II has judged it necessary to circle the wagons around Vatican certainties. On the human level he is undoubtedly right, and God seems to be humble enough to join us there in our need for some certainties. I just don't think it approaches the depth and power of biblical faith. I am not as humble or patient as God.

There has to be solid ground, trust, shared security—or we cannot move outward. There has to be a foundational hope, and for hope to be a shared experience there must be agreed-upon meanings and shared stories that excite and inspire us all. If these are truly stories from the Great Patterns that are always true, they will catapult us into a universal humanity, a pluralistic society, where we can both stand on solid ground and from that solid ground create common ground. *If it does not move us outward, then it is not solid ground at all.*

This is the difference between a mere loyalist and a Great Soul. Obedience to norms is not the same as "the obedience of faith" (Romans 1:5). Loyalty to norms prefers order; faith operates in chaos. We need them both because they need one another to work. But the second is the more necessary for any creative or new future. And that seems to be where God's Word is always leading us.

The Gift of Confidence

Civilization's greatness has emerged from great minds, creativity, saints, inventions. Often it emerges, not surprisingly, in a period of disruption and even chaos. But greatness also emerges when, above all else, people are *confident*. When we believe—together—that life is good, God is good and humanity is good, we become very safe and salutary people for others. We do exciting and imaginative things because we are confident that we are a part of a story line that is going somewhere and we want to be connected to something good.

Many people appreciated Kenneth Clark and his great study of the rise and fall of civilizations. It was made into a popular PBS series some years back. He said at that time, "Civilizations emerge as great civilizations precisely when people are confident." In many ways that's what we lack now. We lack it individually, we lack it corporately, we lack it as a Church, as a nation. We are not a confident people. In fact I'd say almost the opposite: We suffer an immense lack of confidence that we stand for anything beyond the market, that we *are* anything beyond accidents. That this is leading to something good or worthwhile.

The puzzling question, of course, is how do you *create* confidence in a time of no confidence? What are the circumstances that conspire to create a confident era and a confident people? Surely they are so many and so complex that we would call their coming together a "gift of God." We know that we cannot orchestrate a *zeitgeist* on our own.

Theologically speaking, we would say that the virtues of "faith, hope, and love are a participation in the very Life of God." We don't really build up to it, we fall into it. It is not occasioned by perfect circumstances, in fact, most of the people I know who have great faith or hope live in very difficult circumstances. Folks who live in ease, conversely, often have very little faith or hope.

Confidence is really a blending of both faith and hope together. I don't understand the alchemy of that union of substances, but I know when it is there and when it isn't. It often feels like something I have accidentally collapsed into, something that was given from nowhere, something that is a participation in Someone Else. It is of an entirely different nature than natural virtues like temperance or modesty, which we gain by practice or exercise. I think that is why we pray for hope, wait for it, believe in it, leaving the ground fallow until it comes. But those who do such things, *know* that it does come and is always given. And all they can do is thank Someone.

I think we have to pray at this time for the gift of a shared confidence, that deep, gifted stream that has nothing to do with everything going well, but descends from the heavens like the new Jerusalem, "as beautiful as a bride all dressed for her husband" (Revelation 21:3).

Christian hope is different from optimism. Optimism is a natural virtue and a wonderful gift of temperament when things are going well, when you think tomorrow is going to be better than today. Christian hope has nothing to do with the belief that tomorrow is necessarily going to be better than today. The bride is present and that is enough reason for a foundational happiness, even if all else is falling apart. Jesus seems to be saying that if even one mustard seed is blooming, or one dime found, or one sheep recovered—that is enough reason for a big party! (See Luke 15.) Even a small indicator of God is still an indicator of God—and therefore an indicator of reason, meaning and final joy. A little bit of God goes a long way.

CHAPTER SIX

Getting a Whole New Head

· · · · · · · · · · · · · · · ·

IN ORDER TO reconstruct, we need to be open to something more than cerebral, rational knowing. We need to move toward a more spacious, contemplative knowing. We need to move beyond the dualistic seesaw mind to a mind beyond quick judgments, beyond the self and its own self-interest, beyond win/lose and either/or worldviews. This is actually conversion in its most basic sense, but it is also the way to enormous wisdom and the vision of God. Only the whole self is ever ready for the Whole God.

There are many ways of "knowing" reality. Others might use a different or broader description, but I'm going to describe seven here. By ways of knowing I mean *"How* we come to see what we see." It was traditionally the beginning course in all philosophy studies and went by the unfamiliar word *epistemology.* It was the first course we seminarians took in our four years of philosophy studies. You had to reflect on *how* you knew, before you could clearly see *what* you knew which was called "metaphysics." You had to recognize your own lenses and biases before you described what you saw, or we could not trust what you said you saw. Even if the word *epistemology* is no longer a well-known word, the clarity that it offers is more needed than ever because we have many lenses, most of which are largely unowned and unknown. To be honest, Buddhists tend to make their people much more aware of these lenses than most Christians today, especially since humility and detachment are no longer virtues much admired in the West. Early stage religion *must* be about cleaning these lenses, as Teresa of Avila says about the first room in the Interior Castle. Otherwise, there are no other rooms to be entered.

I could never treat the seven ways of knowing adequately in this brief chapter, but I'm going to describe them in quick, surely over-simplified form. More than anything else I hope to help you clean your own lenses so you can really take in the message of this book and, more importantly, the gospel. Like all stories on conversion and transformation, we must begin by admitting that we need a whole new head! And it will take major surgery to cut off the old one, which we thought was the only one.

Intellect

The lens that we most associate with knowing is *intellectual* knowing. It's the result of education, formal education in particular. It has something to do with science, reason and logic and what we call intelligence. Today, it is also common to speak of left-brain knowledge, knowing facts and figures and information. And that's a good way to know. We're grateful for it. Most of us are trained to think that it is the only way of knowing, even the superior way of knowing. Yet that isn't necessarily true. Seeing intellectual intelligence as the best or only way of knowing is actually a great limitation. Daniel Goleman's groundbreaking book, *Emotional Intelligence* (Bantam Books, 1997), has demonstrated this in a rather convincing way. In fact, mere intellectual gray matter is often an actual liability in the real world.

The "absent-minded professor," the "nerd" and the "academic" are contemporary terms indicating this now-apparent limitation. Yet during my time in the seminary (1950's-1960's) this was the attribute that was most trained and most admired and most ordained—even among Franciscans who should have known better! For the most part we were trained to be academics, not pastoral workers. We learned Latin and Greek to connect with ideas and the past; not Spanish or native languages to help us connect with actual people now. Intellectual knowing has all sorts of biases, but never needs to own them because it thinks of itself as so "smart."

Will

The second way of knowing is *volitional* knowing. That's the kind of knowing that comes from making choices, commitments, decisions and sticking with them, and tasting them at different stages. Anyone who has kept vows knows what I'm talking about. The reason you marry and the reason you stay married are not the same reason. In fact, your reasons can change each year, perhaps even each month. It's the same for those of us who keep religious vows. The reason we first take them and the reason we continue in vows changes as we grow. It is a knowing that comes from choices and the very process of struggling with the choices.

This knowing is a kind of cumulative knowing that emerges over time. It is the experiential knowing that comes from staying in the trenches over a period of choices, disillusionments and re-choosings. It is closer to wisdom than mere informational knowledge, but not of itself wisdom. We might choose and re-choose for some very bad or inferior motives. We might decide out of fear, anger or vengeance. This is *willful* knowing (coming from the ego-driven agenda), as opposed to *willing* knowing (coming from surrender and trust). Gerald May understands and explains these two different kinds of will brilliantly (see especially *Will & Spirit*, Harper and Row, 1982). Like no other author I know, he puts together spirituality with very good psychology, without sacrificing either.

Examine your own life. Maybe you made a decision, and after you made the decision you looked at reality differently. You look out from a new viewpoint. The marriage decision is probably the biggest one for most people. But there are certainly many others. What lifestyle will you aspire to? Where will you live? What type of work will you do happily? After making conscious decisions in these big areas, you ask different questions of life. You taste reality at a different level. You will "know" in a new and potentially insightful way.

To have decided for something at ever-deeper levels of free choice is to be a grounded and usually a very alive person. The Franciscan Blessed John Duns Scotus felt that volitional knowing, will, was actually higher and closer to love than intellectual knowing. This always distinguished the Franciscan school from the Dominican Thomists who gave a primacy to knowledge. I am a Scotist because John Duns Scotus was building on Francis' primacy of love over knowledge.

Emotion

Emotional knowing certainly has not been appreciated by the intelligentsia and not by the Church in many ways. As mentioned above, Daniel Goleman demonstrates that it is great to have both a good IQ and a good EQ (emotional quotient), but actually if you have to choose between the two, EQ is a higher indicator of success in life, job and relationships than IQ!

Great emotions are especially powerful teachers. I'm so aware of this in the experience of grief, after the death of my mother a few years back, a teenage niece and my father, more recently.

Even anger and rage are great teachers, if we listen to them. They have so much power to reveal our deepest self to ourselves and to others that we tend to consider them negatively. Yet, they are dangerous and often totally rearrange how we know—or if we know—reality at all. No wonder many even think of anger as a sin.

Such emotions are ways of knowing, believe it or not. They have the capacity to blind you, but also the power to open you up, and bring you to profound conversion, humility and honesty. People who are too nice and never suffer or reveal their own negative emotions, usually do not know very much about themselves—and so the rest of us do not take them too seriously. Consider if that is not true in your own circle of relationships.

Our culture made a sharp split between rational knowing and every other kind of knowing. The first was superior and legitimate knowing; all others were suspect. But I would guess that people die and live much more for emotional knowing than they ever will for rational knowing. Rational knowing really converts no one. If rational knowing is the superior kind, religion has set itself up for major problems. No wonder atheism is a unique problem that emerged in the rational West.

In the past, when people told me about the death of a parent or a loved one, I listened to them and thought I understood them. After I personally had to walk through experiences of death and I experienced this new emotion called grief, I henceforth have lived in a whole new house. I'm in a different space than I had ever experienced before.

Grief work is an essential and central part of men's work, we are finding. Almost all male initiations had to lead men into grief, where they are not at home at all. The feminist movement has rightly recognized that many women, however, have to be led into a necessary anger. Men in our culture consciously avoid the powerlessness of grief; women consciously avoid the not-niceness of anger. But both denials get trapped in the unconscious where they do their dirty work indirectly. We need to know, feel, own and find appropriate expression for our negative as well as our positive emotions.

Love, ecstasy, hatred, jealousy, fear, despair, anguish: each have their lessons. To taste these emotions is to afterwards live in a new reality with a new ability to connect. We can all tell when someone has emotional knowledge of a thing, as opposed to mere head knowledge.

Many today speak of being out of touch or disconnected from our emotional life. It is always a prelude to other problems, or at least a significant loss-of-reality contact.

On a recent trip to India, I twice heard the same quote, "There are no atheists in India." It's little surprise that many of the temple services were also filled with groaning, tears, sensuous dance, waving hands and ecstatic prostrations. We had best not call them merely emotional religions, especially when we see the exodus to the charismatic and Pentecostal forms of Christianity. The feelings also—can and must know God. I fear that many of my seminary professors are going to be wallflowers in the great dance of heaven. They will have nothing to figure out any more, only a party to enter into.

Senses

Bodily or sensory knowing comes through the senses, by touching, moving, smelling, seeing, hearing, breathing, tasting—and especially at a deep or unconscious level. Becoming aware of your senses in a centered way allows you to awaken, to listen, to connect. It allows you to know reality more deeply, on your body's terms instead of your brain's terms.

Recently I gave a yoga retreat in which I talked and a friend, Jim Reale, led the participants in body and breath experiences of what I had just spoken. I felt the message went far deeper than usual, and the prayer had a reality to it that was grounded and heartfelt. Maybe all my retreats should be yoga retreats, yet that very word would scare many Christians away. Many of us like it all in the head where it is nonthreatening and we are in charge of agreeing or disagreeing.

We sometimes speak of "kinesthetic knowing," which might be available to a dancer or long-distance runner, and "corporeal knowing," which can be spoken of in the context of childbirth and lovemaking. In fact, the Hebrew language describes lovemaking as "knowing" the other person.

Many teachers of contemplative prayer find that breathing exercises are the surest way for some people to know God in their bodies. It is no surprise that Jesus touched most people he healed. Something very different is communicated and known through physical touch than what is communicated through mere words. Strange that there is much more New Testament evidence for the washing of the feet as a sacrament than for Holy Orders, but we deemphasized the mandated foot washing (Mark 14:9 and John 13:15) in favor of Holy Orders. And until recently, the bishop even wore white gloves when he did that!

I can from here look out my front window to where we have constructed a seven-cycle labyrinth, with seven 180-degree turns—a turn each time we face an arm of the cross laid out on the ground. Just this morning, a middle-aged Franciscan who is making a directed retreat with me was walking it quite deliberately. When I walked out to talk to him afterwards, he had tears in his eyes that he did not understand. The very walking led him to a knowing too deep for words. That's when tears take over. Tears were called a gift of the Holy Spirit by many of the ancient teachers in the Church, especially the Syrian Fathers. They are surely a deep entranceway into knowing that is both cleansing and softening. Saint Ephrem said that you do not know God until you have cried.

Images

Next, I will speak of imaginative or imaginal knowing. Imaginal knowing, the only way that the unconscious can move into consciousness, happens through fantasy, through dreams, through symbols where all is "thrown together" (*sym-ballein*). It happens through pictures, through events and through well-told stories. It happens through poetry, the well-chosen words that create the image that in turn creates a new awareness—that was in us already. We knew it but we didn't know it. It was in the unconscious, as we say, and needed to be pulled out. It seems that the right-brain and the unconscious do not know conceptually, but through images. Thus people will often break into tears at a picture, a movie, or a human event, much more often than at an idea.

In the Catholic tradition we have a strong sense of the sacramental nature of the world. We know spiritual things by analogy, metaphor, symbol, sign. In fact, it is the only way that we can know spiritual reality. Moses must turn away when God passes by because God can only be known indirectly (Exodus 33:23).

Perhaps the Achilles heel of Protestant theology, largely owing to the period of history in which it emerged, is that it tries to find truth far too much in words, preaching and correct ideas. No wonder that there are now at least five thousand Protestant denominations, and growing. Words are simply too brittle, narrow and culturally trapped to ever be a broad or solid basis for unity. As C. G. Jung puts it, "literalism is always the death of the religious instinct." That is certainly true.

We must be open to imaginal knowing because this work of reconstruction is not going to be done logically, rationally or cerebrally. That mode of knowing is simply not adequate to the greatness and the depth of the task. Remember, imagination is "intellect and will squared." Once you touch the way people *imagine a situation*, change will happen easily and naturally. That is why Jesus told stories to help people *re-imagine* their lives and their relationship with the universe. Once the overall gestalt switches, thinking and feeling change almost immediately.

Recently, a Vietnam veteran who had been decorated for killing many innocent people in Vietnam came to me in tears after seeing a dead body in a ditch. Thirty years later, he got it, not through thousands of sermons, but through a reconfigured and re-membered image of the horror of death. Maybe all true knowing is re-membering, putting the members and memories together in a new and now significant story.

We can't control or manufacture these images. We're going to have to allow the images to show themselves. As Teresa of Avila put it, there are at least two wells in the life of prayer: The first well we have to dig ourselves and keep the trenches flowing toward it. For the second and better well, we just "wait until it bubbles up." That's contemplation, where you get the false self out of the way and the gift shows itself like an apparition. These gifts from the second well have a more personal character. They are usually attached to a symbol and filled with unexplainable energy. It is seldom a verbal locution or clear concept. Thus there is a common need for a guide, a teacher, an interpreter of dreams at this level. It's also why one picture or poem or gnarl of a tree can blow you away when you are truly centered or at prayer.

In some ways we taught sacramental theology, but the truly sacramental is in fact scary and inherently in God's hands. In a sense, we tried to limit God to Seven Sacraments and clearly defined all the hows, whens, whos and wheres. A sacramental way of life can and will really change us, but most of us don't really want to go into the unknown or leave God in the hands of amateurs. It is no surprise that we have avoided images in favor of concepts, personal faith journeys in favor of boxed-in sacraments. The "tabernacle" of Exodus was on the move, leading the people through the desert. Now the tabernacle must, by order of Canon Law (#938), be "immovable," that is, be nailed or bolted down. What a different idea!

It is interesting to me that Iconoclasm (the destruction of images) was a central issue in two major schisms within Church history: in the East in the eighth and ninth centuries, and in the West at the time of the Reformation. Protestantism has never totally recovered from such left-brain fury. You know you are dealing with something archetypal and powerful when the human psyche reacts to such a violent degree. Catholics probably kept images domesticated by the mass production of sentimental, saccharine and anglicized images of all the great mysteries. Perhaps we killed the imaginal mind by pretending to honor it.

Aesthetic

That leads us to the next distinct kind of knowing. In some ways, aesthetic knowing is the most attractive, but I think it's the least converting.

It's close to knowing and it can be a kind of knowing, but aesthetic knowing is either so pretty or so ugly that we tend to stop there. Art in all its forms so engages you and satisfies you that many go no deeper. The aesthete and the dilettante think because they've tasted the picture or the poem or the wonderful piece of sculpture that, in fact, they've changed their lives or experienced true transcendence. Usually aesthetic knowing is only an entranceway, but it is indeed a way of knowing, too.

This art for art's sake attitude was part of the reason for the needed reaction of the Protestant reformers. Just tour many of the "gilded lily" churches of Europe—paintings from floor to ceiling, and monuments to bishops and popes. I cannot imagine this centering anyone on God or on anything except, "Aren't we wonderful." Baroque and Rococo churches were supposed to bring people back to Catholicism. They might well have done that, but I doubt whether they brought them back to the gospel. Aesthetics don't always demand transformation or increase real knowing, and often become a seductive substitute for the same. Thus we have the revealing words *connoisseur* (from the French for knowing "thoroughly"), or *dilettante* (from the Italian for an "amateur" who thinks he is not), or an *epicurean* who thinks that "the best" is in fact the best.

People who espouse aesthetic knowing play around superficially with profound ideas and beauty, but they may never move toward substance. Aesthetic knowing never hits their politics, it never changes their attitude toward the poor. It is all posturing and posing. Aesthetics can be a way of knowing, but it can also be an avoidance of knowing. Picasso's *Guernica* told us something profound about the evil of violence. The popular movie *Pulp Fiction*, conversely, trivializes, normalizes and cheapens the evil of violence.

Image can get in the way of substance. Ritual can be an avoidance of reality, as the Mass itself sometimes has become. The Japanese people seem seldom to ask questions of metaphysics or religion, yet they are some of the most highly ritualized people in the world. Good and ubiquitous ritual can dull and substitute for the authentic religious drive.

Still, aesthetic knowing is a central and profound way of knowing. Maybe it is open to misuse precisely because it is so powerful. I've seen art lead to true changes of consciousness. I have seen people change their lives in response to a novel, a play, a piece of music or a movie like *Dead Man Walking*. Their souls were prepared and God got in through "the right metaphor at the right time." They saw their own stories clarified inside of a larger story line.

Epiphany

The last way of knowing and the one you'd think religion would prefer and encourage is "epiphanic knowing." An epiphany is a parting of the veil, a life-changing manifestation of meaning, the eureka of awareness of self and the Other. It is the radical grace, which you cannot manufacture or orchestrate. There are no formulas which ensure its appearance. It is always a gift unearned and unexpected and larger than one's present life.

It happens in most unusual settings, usually non-religious settings, often a needed sign that you didn't cause it yourself by devotion or morality. I have met very few people who have had their great conversions inside churches or during liturgies, for example. You cannot manufacture epiphanies. You can only ask for them, wait for them, expect them, know they are given, keep out of the way and thank Someone afterwards.

PART TWO

Francis the Rebuilder

Help Us to Hope

*O loving God, we thank you for bringing us the rivers
and streams of this world. May the rivers we know
be an image of the stream that you want to flow
within each one of us. Teach us now, take away all fear,
dare to let us believe that we could really be a small part
of a reconstructed society, that we could build again.
Take away our own cynicism. Take away our lack of hope.
Take away our own anger and judgments. We thank you
for the faith and the desire that is in our hearts. You
have planted it there. Now help us to preserve it, protect
it and increase it. We long for vision, Lord. We need
vision and we know we will perish without it. Help us
open each new day to a new meaning, to a new hope, to
a deeper desiring. Show us your face, loving God, and
we will be satisfied. We ask for all of this in Jesus' name.
Amen.*

CHAPTER SEVEN

Francis of Assisi:
Showing the Way Toward
Reconstruction

· · · · · · · · · · · · · ·

IN THE THIRTEENTH CENTURY, in a dilapidated chapel on the plain below a fortress city in Italy, a man heard Jesus speak to him from the cross: "Francis, rebuild my church, for you can see it is in ruins." This young man, searching for meaning and beauty in a world that no longer made sense to him, heard the message and, over time, saw a new way of being that would change the face of history.

Beauty hurts, especially for those who have once seen how beautiful it really is. Ugliness irritates, but only for those who have never seen. When the great seers arise, their lives always confuse the rest of us. They seem to change all the rules, look in different directions for joy and find love in the most unexpected places. They are the rebuilders, the reconstructionists.

Those who have seen the full extent of beauty set our minds awhirl; we take centuries to refind our bearings, and meanwhile, chase blinking-eyed after them. Such a seer was Francesco Bernardone (1182-1226), and such a people is the eight hundred years of admiring and unsettled humanity that cannot forget what he saw and what he did with his one little life. His beauty and his seeing still hurt us.

More than any other follower of Christ, Francis of Assisi has been called a "second Christ." According to the Smithsonian bibliography, more lives have been written of him than of any other person. He has been the most painted non-biblical character in history, and the usually cautious Church declared him a saint only four years after his death. G. K. Chesterton called him "the world's one quite sincere democrat," and the "first hero of humanism." Vladimir Lenin spoke envyingly of him shortly before he died, and Sir Kenneth Clark called him Europe's greatest religious genius. Even in his own lifetime Francis exerted a strange attractiveness. Perhaps it was the undeniable magnetism that occurs when truth and folly stand together:

> One day when St. Francis was coming back from the woods, where he had been praying, and was at the edge of the forest, Brother Masseo went to meet him, and said to St. Francis, half-jokingly, "Why after you? Why after you? Why after you? Why does all the world seem to be running after you, and everyone seems to want to see you and hear you and obey you? You are not a handsome man. You do not have great learning or wisdom. You are not a nobleman. So why is all the world running after you?"
>
> Then with great fervor of spirit he turned to Brother Masseo and said: "...I have this from the all-holy eyes of God that see the good and the evil everywhere. For those blessed and all-holy eyes have not seen among sinners anyone more vile or insufficient than I am. And so in order to do that wonderful work which he intends to do, he did not find on earth a more ordinary creature, and therefore he chose me. For God has chosen the foolish things of this world to put to shame the wise, and God has chosen the base things of this world and the despised, to bring to naught the noble, the great and the strong." (*The Little Flowers of St. Francis*)*

Darkness Revealed in the Light

Francis' starting place was utter truth. His prayer for nights on end was simply: "Who are you, O God? And who am I?" He repeated it without ceasing, and the response cited above seems to be his answer. He knew that he was radically unfinished and that he always would be. As he charted his own conversion to the moment when he could embrace an ugly and smelly leper, so his journey in truth began when he could accept the leper part of himself.

He spent much of the rest of his life not hiding or disguising that truth, but actually seeming to advertise it. This deep acceptance of his own limitations and capacity for evil had none of the destructiveness and self-loathing that we often find in ourselves. He only rejoiced in the possibility and promise of their redemption.

Francis' reading of the gospel is of utmost relevance today. His focus and emphasis is the same as Jesus'. His life was an enacted parable, an audiovisual aid to gospel freedom; it gives us the perspective by

---

* All excerpts from sources on the life of Saint Francis in this chapter are taken from *Omnibus of the Sources for the Life of St. Francis*, edited by Marion A. Habig, Franciscan Herald Press, 1972.

which to see as Jesus did: the view from the bottom. He insists by every facet of his life that we can only see rightly from a disestablished position. He wanted to be poor most of all—simply because Jesus was poor.

But he also knew that the biblical promises were made to the poor, that the gospel could be preached only to the poor because they alone had the freedom to hear it without distorting it for their own purposes. He wanted to have nothing to protect except the love that made all else useless. "Love is not loved! Love is not loved!" he used to sigh.

Contrary to the rest of the human race, therefore, he raced in the other direction, certain that he was following the path of Christ. Like Paul, all he wanted was "to know him and the power of his resurrection and to partake of his sufferings by being moulded to the pattern of his death" (Philippians 3:11). He knew there was no life in the secure life at the top. He himself had begun there as the son of a rich cloth merchant, and he saw that much of the Church had been seduced and entrapped into a kind of spiritual materialism, all the more illusory because it appeared to be for the sake of God and the work of the kingdom. He often referred to himself as an *idiota,* but he was not so stupid as to be unable to recognize simple freedom and the lack of it.

Rule of the Gospel

Francis initially needed no rule, no code of behavior, for his brother friars. He was quite satisfied with Jesus' Sermon on the Mount and his instructions to the disciples. But, Saint Bonaventure tells us, as the number of friars increased, and approval from Rome was desired, a more formal rule became necessary. For his rule, he simply connected a series of Gospel quotes together with his own admonitions. This remains the rule of the Friars Minor to this day, and was approved by Pope Honorius III in 1223.

When Francis read the inaugural discourse of Jesus, he saw that the call to be poor stood right at the beginning: "How blessed are the poor in spirit!" Henceforward, Francis' reading of the gospel considered poverty to be "the foundation of all other virtues and their guardian." The other virtues receive the kingdom only in promise; poverty, however, is invested with it already now and without delay. "Theirs is the kingdom of heaven" (Matthew 5:3).

As a result, Franciscan spirituality has never been an abstraction. It is grounded in Jesus' specific instructions to his disciples and not in theology. It is not easily able to move into ideology or to hide behind denominational screens onto which we have projected our own worldviews.

Francis' living of the gospel was just that: It was lifestyle pure and simple. It was the Incarnation continuing in space and time. It was the presence of the Spirit taken absolutely seriously. It was *being* Jesus more than simply worshiping him. At its best, Franciscanism is not words or even ethics. It is flesh—naked flesh—unable to deny its limitations, unable to cover its wounds. He called it poverty.

This pure vision of gospel life attracted thousands to a new freedom in the Church and in ministry. Religious communities had become more and more entangled with stipends, benefices and rich land holdings. Members lived individually simple lives but were corporately secure and even comfortable. The begging, or mendicant, orders were born to break that dangerous marriage between ministry and money. Francis did not want his friars to *preach* salvation (although they did that, too) as much as he wanted them to *be* salvation. He wanted them to model and image the life of Jesus in the world, with all of the trusting and insecurity that would entail.

Today, living this way, we would be arrested as vagrants, but he believed that Jesus meant what he said when he told the disciples to eat whatever is set before you, "for the laborer deserves his wages" (see Luke 10:7). When Francis first heard Jesus' sermon telling his followers to "take nothing for your journey," he left Mass overjoyed and committed the whole passage to memory, saying: "This is what I want. This is what I long for. This is what I desire to do with all my heart."

When I think of the life of Francis, I am reminded of a poor Lutheran pastor and his wife whom I met in a small village in Germany. When he left the room, she spoke of her husband with great love and respect, even though his radical commitment to the gospel had brought her great pain and privation. Before her husband re-entered, she whispered to me solemnly and proudly, "He makes being poor look brilliant! And like brilliance, he lights up everything."

So also Francis was no dark ascetic, but a passionate and sensuous Italian who did not equate poverty with gracelessness or slovenliness. One need only visit his prayer spots throughout central Italy to discover that he chose the most scenic and lovely settings in which to disclose the darkness of his own soul. He knew that he had to surround himself with God's delighting in order to risk such painful truths.

The Poverty of Christ

Francis could not just be poor; he had to have a love affair, and even a marriage, with his beloved, "Lady Poverty." His celibacy had to be a passion, not a lack of it. In the twelfth- and thirteenth-century tradition of courtly love, the sublimated love of a knight for his idealized lady, Francis insisted that he would marry only "the noblest, the richest, the most beautiful woman ever seen." She turned out to be Lady Poverty:

> The blessed father considered the common wealth of the sons of men as trifles, and ambitious for higher things, he longed for Lady Poverty with all his heart. Looking upon poverty as especially dear to the Son of God, though it was spurned throughout the whole world, he sought to espouse it in perpetual charity. Therefore, after he had become a lover of her beauty, he not only left his father and mother, but even put aside all things that he might cling to her more closely as his spouse and that they might be two in one spirit... There was no one desirous of gold as he was desirous of poverty, and no one so solicitous in guarding his treasure as he was solicitous in guarding this pearl of the gospel. (Thomas of Celano, *Second Life of Saint Francis*)

Francis was enough of a realist to know that this view from the bottom would never become fashionable. Yet his commitment to lowliness led him to name his brothers "minors" so that they would never fall back again into the worldview of the "majors" (the great, the nobility). He knew that there was power in being a somebody, but that there was truth in being a nobody. He always opted for the truth and, from the example of Jesus crucified, knew that the Lord would create a new kind of power from those who hold together the tension of opposites: human and divine, spirit and flesh, male body and female soul, sadness and utter joy. The price of such holding is always crucifixion.

He was astonishingly unimpressed by numbers, success, degrees and status symbols. Seeking humility, he refused to be ordained a priest. He was not about to be co-opted by any kingdoms less than that of the "Great King." He never railed against the show and trappings of medieval Catholicism; in fact, he loved the Church deeply. He simply moved outside the walls of Assisi and did it in a new way. He knew that frontal attacks never work anyway, and he loved the Church too much to presume to judge the others. Again, it was his lifestyle that shouted judgment, not his words. He was a gentle prophet. His witness, therefore, has been able to call and challenge believers for eight centuries hence.

Francis' choice of weakness instead of strength, vulnerability instead of righteousness, truth instead of practicality, honesty instead of influence stands in amazing contrast to the general Westernized version of the gospel, and to the success-oriented and electronic Church so readily received today. He is forever the saint of "holy topsy-turvey-dom," as Chesterton said.

Heart of the Gospel

Francis seemed to have very little conscious awareness of what we would today call corporate or systemic evil. At least he did not consciously speak of his mission in that light. Yet if his interpretation of the gospel had been taken as foundational instead of merely admired and then marginalized, one can only imagine the different color and character of Western Christianity and civilization today.

If greed and power and control had been recognized as the demons they are, if spiritual goods could have been fittingly valued, the Renaissance could have been for real, the Reformation might not have been necessary, the Enlightenment could have moved beyond the mind, and the individual and the class warfare called for by Marxism would not have been necessary.

Because most of the Church has refused to take Jesus' teaching and Francis' example seriously, now much of the world refuses to take Christians seriously. People may say: "You Christians love to talk of a new life, but the record shows that you are afraid to live in a new way—a way that is responsible, caring and making for peace."

Living in a feudal period of history, Francis had no knowledge of the monstrous proportions that our love of war would attain, but in his own limited world, he abandoned his early life as a knight and warrior, even though this career was very esteemed and culturally approved. He applied that same knightly chivalry and courage to the local battles for goodness. In their greeting the Friars Minor were to announce their purpose:

> The Lord revealed to me that I should say as a greeting, "The Lord give you peace." And one day when he was traveling along the road with another friar, the friar used his greeting of peace. And because people had never heard such a greeting from any religious, they were very startled. Indeed, some said indignantly, "What do you mean by this greeting of yours?" As a result the friar became embarrassed, and said to Francis, "Allow us to use some other greeting." But the Holy Father said, "Let them chatter, for they do not understand the ways of God. Don't feel ashamed because of this, for one day the nobles and princes of this world will respect you and the other friars for this greeting.

For it is no marvel if the Lord should desire to have a new little flock, whose speech and way of life are unlike those of all its predecessors, and which is content to possess him alone." (*The Mirror of Perfection*)

And centuries later the Church is still calling forth embarrassingly little flocks to speak the gospel of peace, while the nobles and princes of this world are still withholding their respect. The saints of every age must learn to trust in invisible victories—victories outside of history. They accept ahead of time that this "kingdom" will always disappoint them, but that does not make it any less the Reign of God. Even one true moment of peace is enough to prove that God *is*, and that we can live in joy and contentment now.

Women of Poverty and Contemplation

Perhaps no one understood the vision and vocation of Francis better than a young, wealthy woman of Assisi named Clare di Offreduccio (1194-1253). She took the call of gospel poverty to her heart like no other. Of Francis she said, "After God he is the charioteer of my soul." She received from Innocent III in 1216 and from Gregory IX in 1228 her famous "Privilege of Poverty." It took two papal pronouncements to protect and assure a religious community that they would be allowed to live in insecurity. Clare knew that wise and prudent people would try to take away what she saw as essential to gospel life.

It is generally agreed that the female branch of the Franciscan family has likely lived the poverty and contemplation of Francis much more faithfully than have the friars. Many reasons could probably be given for this, but the most obvious is that the men have been used for religious function and jurisdiction in the institutional Church, which invariably takes away one's appreciation of lifestyle and prayer as ends in themselves. We often became such "company men" that we lost the freedom to speak prophetically to that company. Soon after Francis' death the Order became clericalized, with faculties and privilege. We, in great part, lost the bias from the bottom and the privileged perspective from the side of the poor. We lost, in a sense, by succeeding so well. One wonders if that was not Francis' greatest fear.

Unfortunately, the Poor Clares have had to remain in a cloister to retain their privileged vantage point. Maybe there is no other way. History has shown us how rare it is for people to be both in the world and yet not of the world, as Jesus has called us. Even though few seem to attain this balance, it will always remain the Franciscan ideal. The greatest vocation is not the contemplative, nor is it the active, but the utter art form of putting the two together.

Franciscans have usually been seen as "of the people." Our self-image is one of "blue-collar clergy" instead of white-collar or clerical-collar professionals. This has allowed the friars to be in closer touch with the concerns of ordinary folk, but sometimes out of touch with good and corrective thinking. As always, one's gift is one's liability. The friars have often reflected the common folks' prejudices and fears as much as they have reflected their concerns for justice and compassion.

Peacemaker at Home

Francis saw himself as a reconciler and preacher of forgiveness. After a longstanding quarrel between the mayor and the bishop of Assisi, he decided to add another verse to his famous *Canticle of Brother Sun*. Even here there was no room in his spacious heart for harsh epithets or cruel judgments. He had seen too much beauty. He hurt when others hurt. And even his reconciliations took the form of art and courtesy in what is considered to be the first piece of Italian poetry.

> It is a great shame for us, the servants of God, that at a time when the [mayor] and the bishop so hate each other no one can be found to re-establish peace and concord between them," said Francis to his companions. And so he added a further strophe to his *Canticle of Brother Sun*:

> All praise be yours, my Lord,
> Through those who grant pardon for love of you;
> Through those who endure trial and persecution.
> Happy those who endure in peace;
> By you, Most High, they will be crowned.

> And the friars went to the Piazza Commune and sang their canticle in the presence of the mayor and the bishop. And "with much tenderness and affection they both locked arms and embraced each other." (*The Legend of Perugia*)

Peacemaking Abroad: Francis and the Sultan

In the times of Francis "not only had war and its orgies and disorders become a necessity and a habit, but they had become the preferred occupation, the ruling passion, and the whole life of the city, in which 'peace' no longer had any meaning" (*Nova Vita di san Francesco*, Arnaldo Fortini). Undoubtedly the most famous of Francis' ventures into peacemaking was his personal visit with the sultan Melek-el-Khamil (1217-1238) at Damietta in Egypt.

The crusaders had been fighting from May 9, 1218, until August 29, 1219, the very day when Francis arrived in Egypt. He spent several days with the sultan trying to arrange a peace, but only gained his personal respect. He turned then to the Christian crusaders:

> "If I tell them not to fight, I will be considered a fool; if I am silent, I will not escape my conscience." And so the holy man arose and approached the Christians with salutary warnings, forbidding the war, denouncing the reason for it. But truth was turned to ridicule, and they hardened their heart and refused to be guided. They went, they joined the battle, they fought and our [sic] army was pressed hard by the enemy. So great was the number of soldiers lost in the disaster that six thousand were among the dead and captured. Compassion pressed upon the holy man, even though they were not regretful over the deed. He mourned especially over the Spaniards, when he saw how their great impetuosity had left but a few of them remaining. Let the princes of this world know these things and let them know that it is not easy to fight against God, against the will of the Lord. Rashness generally ends in disaster, for it relies on its own power and does not deserve help from heaven. But if victory is to be hoped for from on high, battles must be entrusted to the Spirit of God. (Thomas of Celano, *Second Life*)

Unfortunately, history tells us that fighting resumed on September 26, and Francis returned to Assisi a very discouraged man. Yet his warnings to his followers are apt for peacemakers and those working for justice in our day:

> "While you are proclaiming peace with your lips, be careful to have it even more fully in your heart. Nobody should be roused to wrath or insult on your account. Everyone should rather be moved to peace, goodwill, and mercy as a result of your self-restraint. For we have been called for the purpose of healing the wounded, binding up those who are bruised, and reclaiming the erring." (*The Legend of the Three Companions*)

Many historians consider Francis' rule of life for laypeople one of the major contributing factors to the death of feudalism. Feudalism was a system based on oppression and control. Feuds and vendettas were so common that few people went abroad unarmed. Yet Francis forbade his followers to fight, carry weapons or even swear allegiance to any noble. This was based, of course, in Jesus' teaching from the Sermon on the Mount. So many thousands of people committed themselves to this Third Order Rule that it was one of the world's few successful nonviolent reforms, even if rather short-lived. Soon even the secular Franciscans represented the systems of power more than providing an alternative to them. Devotions *to* Saint Francis were a lot easier than actually doing what Saint Francis did. It seems to be the perennial temptation of religion: to worship instead of imitate. Yet Jesus said "follow me," not "worship me."

Man of Joy

Despite all of his legitimate reasons for discouragement, Francis was known as a man of deep and abiding joy. He knew that after all was done and undone, he was still "the herald of the Great King." No one should ever doubt that Francis was quintessentially a man in love, and a man in love with the greatest of lovers. There was simply no bottom to his grateful happiness. He told his friars that it was their vocation "to lift up peoples' hearts and give them reasons for spiritual joy."

They needed no other justification for their life. They needed no other ministry in the Church. They, like he, were to be troubadours and minstrels of the Lord. At times, eyewitnesses tell us that he was so filled with gladness that "he would pick up a stick from the ground and putting it over his left arm, would draw across it, as across a violin, a little bow bent by means of a string; and going through the motions of playing, he would sing about the Lord. This whole ecstasy of joy would often end in tears and would be dissolved in compassion" (Thomas of Celano's *Second Life*). To communicate this wisdom of the heart to his community, he engaged Brother Leo in one of his most quoted stories, the dialogue of perfect joy:

> One winter day when he and Brother Leo were walking along the road to Assisi from Perugia, Francis called out to Leo in the bitter cold five times, each time telling him what perfect joy was not: "Brother Leo, even if a Friar Minor gives sight to the blind, heals the paralyzed, drives out devils, gives hearing back to the deaf, makes the lame walk, and restores speech to the dumb, and what is more brings back to life a man who has been dead four

days, write that perfect joy is not in that." And so he continued with different enumerations of success and even spiritual enjoyment. And when he had been talking this way for a distance of two miles, Brother Leo in great amazement asked him: "Father, I beg you in God's name to tell me where perfect joy is then to be found?"

And Francis replied: "When we come to the Portiuncula, soaked by the rain and frozen by the cold, all soiled with mud and suffering from hunger, and we ring at the gate of our friary and the brother porter comes and says angrily: 'Who are you?' And we say: 'We are two of your brothers.' And he contradicts us, saying, 'You are not telling the truth. Go away!' And he does not open for us, but makes us stand outside in the snow and rain, cold and hungry until night falls—then if we endure all of those insults and cruel rebuffs patiently, without being troubled and without complaining, and if we reflect humbly and lovingly that the porter really knows us. Oh, Brother Leo, write that perfect joy is to be found there!

"And if we continue to knock and the porter comes out and drives us away with curses and hard blows and if we bear it patiently and take the insults with joy and love in our hearts. Oh, Brother Leo, write down that this is perfect joy! And now hear the conclusion: Above all the graces and gifts of the Holy Spirit which Christ gives to his friends is that of conquering oneself and willingly enduring sufferings, insults, humiliations, and hardships for the love of Christ." (*The Little Flowers of St. Francis*)

Now that is an alternative universe! In one frightening story, he has realigned all of our usual responses, our loyalties, and the very shape of reality as most of us have designed it. Clearly this is a different kind of "I" that is speaking here, an "I" hidden with Christ in God (Colossians 3:3). This is the goal of all transformation and journeys toward holiness.

The Freedom of Rebuilders

This is not so much a description of perfect joy as it is a description of perfect freedom. Here at last we have a truly nonviolent and liberated man. Only such as these will ever liberate others. They are not part of the problem, but most assuredly the beginnings of the solution. They have moved beyond here and there, mine and yours, beyond all manner of divisions, to recognize, as Gerard Manley Hopkins describes, the "dearest freshness, deep down things."

They seem to accept without despair that we are together in one another's sin, and they seem to honestly enjoy one another's glories. Every part really is trying to love every other part—but with great struggle and obstacles unlimited. Some few people become points where all the parts can meet. And these rare jigsaw pieces of persons hold the rest of the puzzled picture together. They give us both cause for sanity and excuses for outrageous adventure. But to do that for us they must become small enough so that none of us are threatened, so that we can think we are actually giving instead of receiving.

These free ones must be the rejoicing of God. These few tell us what is going on inside the heart of God. These few reassure us that whoever this Creator is, God is most assuredly not omnipotence, but humility, not lordly (as God should be), but infinitely accessible, not withholding, but relentlessly welcoming. And in their flesh they try to imitate God in an amazingly non-Utopian way because they are ready to live it in any circumstances whatsoever.

For those like Francis of Assisi goodness has come to be expected, goodness is no surprise, goodness always finally happens, goodness seems to be willing to suffer in order to win, but win it does. For these few free ones, goodness is just there, everywhere, right beneath the surface and quite often breaking through. They cannot resist it nor totally possess it. So they adore. And because they have bowed down, the ugliness of life can attract them, and the beauty of it all is a strange and sacred hurt.

Francis the Rebuilder

Probably one of the most quoted lines of Francis is attributed to his final days. He told the friars toward the end of his life, "Let us begin again, for up to now we have done nothing." That enigmatic sense of beginning again at the end of life, at the end of an era, in the middle of so much failure, when you just want to rest and put the past behind you, that is the gift for reconstruction that we want to discover in this book. It makes Francis a man for all seasons, but surely for seasons of winter and death, when we do not know how, much less want, to begin again.

Most simply and yet most difficultly, Francis is first of all saying that *we cannot change the world except insofar as we have changed ourselves*. We can only give away who we are. We can only offer to others what God has done in us. We have no real head answers. We must be an answer. We only know the other side of journeys that we have made ourselves. Francis walked to the edge and so he could lead others to what he found there.

All the conflicts and contradictions of life must find a resolution in us before we can resolve anything out there. Only the forgiven can forgive, only the healed can heal, only those who stand daily in need of mercy can offer mercy to others. At first it sounds simplistic and even individualistic, but it is precisely such people who can finally effect profound and long-lasting social change.

It has something to do with what we now call quantum theology. The cosmos is mirrored in the microcosmos. If we let the mystery happen in one small and true place, it moves from there! It is contagious, it is shareable, it reshapes the world. Thus both Jesus and Francis had no pragmatic agenda for social reform. They just moved *outside the system of illusion, more ignoring it than fighting it* and quite simply doing it better. They knew, again, that: *the best criticism of the bad is the practice of the better.* They moved to a much larger place that we call holiness/wholeness in God, and from there could deal kindly with all smaller places. Nothing threatened them; everything elated them, reflecting their own infinite abundance.

Don't waste any time dividing the world into the good guys and the bad guys. *Hold them both together in your own soul—where they are anyway—and you will have held together the whole world.* You will have overcome the great divide—in one place of spacious compassion. You, little you, will have paid the price of redemption. God takes it from there, but always by replicating the same pattern in another conscious human life.

God does all the patient work and we get all the saintly credit. Only the chosen ones know the big and well-hidden secret: We really are chosen because we are nothing, and we know it. Maybe that's what it means to be chosen. All the unchosen ones think it has something to do with worthiness and merit. Francis was clearly a chosen one, and the precise vocation of a chosen one is to communicate to others this big, hidden secret.

PART THREE
Finding a Third Way

Prayer for Presence

Let us be present to the now. It's all we have and it's where God will always speak to us. The now holds everything, rejects nothing and, therefore, can receive God, too. Help us be present to the place we're most afraid of, because it always feels empty, it always feels boring, it always feels like it's not enough. Help us find some space within that we don't try to fill with ideas or opinions. Help us find space so you, loving God, can show yourself in that place where we are hungry and empty. Keep us out of the way, so there is always room enough for you.

Good God, we believe that you are here and your presence gives us hope. We thank you for each day of our lives. We thank you for so many further chances to understand, to forgive again, to trust again and to love. We thank you that we live now, that our problems are soul-sized. We ask that you teach us and lead us, that you put the thoughts into our mind that you want us to think, the feelings in our hearts that you want us to feel. Reconstruct us, Lord. Put us together because we don't know how to do it ourselves. We trust that you are hearing this prayer, and that you care for the answer more than we do. We pray therefore not alone, but with the whole body of Christ in Jesus' name. Amen.

CHAPTER EIGHT

What Is Your Window on Reality?

. . . .

EVERYBODY LOOKS at the world through their own lens, a matrix of culturally inherited qualities, family influences and other life experiences. This lens, or worldview, truly determines what you bring to every discussion. When Jesus spoke of the coming of the Reign of God, he was trying to change peoples' foundational worldview. When Francis spoke of his marriage to Lady Poverty, he was using a lovely metaphor to describe his central thesis for life. When Americans speak of money as "the bottom line," they are revealing more about their real worldview than they realize.

We would do well to get in touch with our own operative worldview. It is there anyway, so you might as well know what this highly influential window on reality is. It's what really motivates you. Your *de facto* worldview determines what you pay attention to and what you don't notice at all. It's largely unconscious and it drives you to do this and not that. It is surely important to become conscious of such a primary lens, or we will never know what we *don't* see and why we see other things out of all perspective.

Until we can allow the gospel to move into that deepest level of the unconscious and touch our operative worldviews nothing substantial is going to change. It will only be rearranging the furniture, but not constructing a new room. Conversion is about constructing a new room, or maybe even a whole new house. One wonders if this was not the full meaning of Jesus' words to Francis from the cross at San Damiano: "Rebuild my house, for you see that it is falling into ruins."

I remember the first time I was in an extended hermitage in Kentucky. When I was walking a little path, one of the recluses came walking toward me. Now the recluses are more hermits than hermits! They only come in from their seclusion for events like Holy Week and

Christmas—and all the monks are waiting to see if they are glowing or crazy! I knew who this hermit was. I'd heard of him as a former abbot. I was excited that I would get to see this holy man, and I didn't want to break his reclusiveness, so I said nothing. But he apparently knew I was on the grounds. He said to me, as he pointed upward, "Richard, when you preach, be sure to keep telling the people, '*God is not out there!*' Thank you." And then he went on down the road.

That recluse had the worldview that I would call truly Christian, Incarnational. It is actually not too common, even among baptized Christians. The vast majority of Christians I have met worldwide are actually theists, but not Incarnational at all. God is still *out* there, invited *into* things, and they are all inviting God to come *to* them. Theism, the most common form of religion, is still a split worldview. True Christianity is totally integrative. There is one world, all supernatural, and God comes *through* us, not to us. It is imaged by Paul as the Body of Christ and by John as the Vine and the Branches. Jesus speaks of "one flock and one shepherd," "abiding in love" or "I and the Father are one."

So few people have experienced this divine image as the innermost possession of their own souls. Christ only meets them from without, never from within. So their operative worldview is still God is out there and we are down here, a three-level universe: Hell, Earth and Heaven. It is always a matter of getting God down here and getting us up there. Actually many, if not most, of the orations in the official *Sacramentary* (prayers for Catholic Eucharist) still reveal this split worldview. And unfortunately in this case, "*lex orandi est lex credendi*": The way we pray shapes the way we believe.

Our operative worldview is formed by three images that are inside every one of us. They are not something from outside. They have already taken shape within us. All we can do is become aware of them, which is to awaken them. The three images to be awakened and transformed are your image of self, your image of God and your image of the world. A true hearing of the gospel transforms those images into a very exciting and, I believe, truthful worldview. When we say Christ is the truth, that's what we mean. Christ renames reality correctly according to what reality honestly is, putting aside whatever we think it is or whatever we fear it is. Reality is always better than any of us imagined or feared; there is joy associated with a true hearing of the gospel.

Normally your worldview answers several foundational questions. The first question that your worldview answers is: "What should be?" Or, "What's your grand and final vision?" That in great part is what we've lost, what should be, what it could be, what the world is supposed to mean. We're almost afraid to believe what should be. We deny, or at least, doubt all shoulds and oughts.

The second has to do with the state of things: "Why are things messed up?" Or, "why do we suffer?" Or, "why are things not the way they should be?" The earliest religions credited this to fussy gods, demanding gods, punishing gods or even toxic gods. God, in general, was not someone you liked. The world, furthermore, was a dangerous place filled with dangerous spirits. That left the individual self-inse-cure, fearful and pleading.

The third question that your worldview answers is: "How do we get from what's broken to what should be?" Or, "How do we live to make things right?" Or quite simply, "What does it mean to be a good human being?"

All together we could put it this way: "What should life be?" "Why isn't it?" "How do we repair it?" When these are answered for us, at least implicitly, we have our game plan and we can live safely and with purpose in this world. Without this game plan, our life is a bad novel with no beginning, middle or end; circular, but not a spiral.

Differing worldviews have their own explanations for suffering and their own ways of trying to resolve it. Some early peoples felt that the explanation for suffering was simply imposition of trials and threats by a fussy and temperamental god. Somehow you had to get this god on your good side by sacrificing a virgin daughter or an eldest son, perhaps by burning them at the stake. We see remnants of this in the Abraham and Isaac story. Somehow suffering and sacrifice were supposed to please an angry god. Often people felt they had to demean or punish themselves to get God to stop punishing them. Literally, you had to beat God to the punch. You can see that many contemporary people have not moved much beyond this worldview. It is a sort of sadomasochistic game of reward and punishment, but still deep in the unconscious of many churchgoing Christians.

The Buddhist worldview would say we suffer because we have too much desire. Spirit is imprisoned inside vicious matter and we must move beyond matter to spirit. The Buddhist goal is Nirvana, freedom from matter, freedom from desire. The solution is meditation, so that we see the truth. And of course they've got something very right. We need to move beyond the shadow and the disguise, something we in the West have not learned very well. For the most part we've avoided the deeper forms of transformative prayer. One of Buddhism's great insights is demonstrated in leading its people to that deeper form of prayer that dislodges the ego and changes the agenda-driven person.

Prayer is not just asking God for things.

The Marxist worldview blames suffering on private property, rich people and greed. There is some truth to that, but Marxism carries it to extremes. The Marxist expounds universal equality through enforced common ownership of all possessions. Once you accept that, you read everything through those eyes. This worldview does address some problems of injustice and inequality, but it creates some new ones. Those who have are usually bad; those who have not are automatically superior. This divides up the good guys and bad guys neatly, but it just ain't that simple. Nor can "virtue" be enforced; if it is enforced, it is not virtue.

The capitalist worldview is a little closer to home for most who might be reading this book. We don't think of capitalism as something to criticize. Yet capitalism offers its own explanations that are less than Christ-like. The capitalist worldview blames suffering on inertia and laziness. Those who are lazy and irresponsible do not achieve capitalism's goal: material prosperity. That's why most analyses in the media are economic analyses. "How's the economy doing?" That's our big question because materialism is our basic mythology. What quickly follows from this worldview is each person for himself or herself and an almost necessary lack of compassion for those left behind. Once competition and success are virtues, not to be competitive or successful is almost sinful.

The postmodern and liberal culture, or worldview, would say the reason we suffer is that we're uptight, that there are too many laws and structures. If there were unlimited freedom for everybody to be true to their deepest feelings and instincts, we'd have a wonderful world. The solution therefore is to rebel and to be true to yourself: "If it feels good, do it." Or, "I must find myself and take care of myself before I can worry about others." The trouble is that people with these concerns never get to others because the ego self is insatiable. Yet this worldview remains largely uncriticized in the sophisticated West.

When you describe these worldviews as crassly as I just did, they sound absurd. Perhaps that can open us to listen to what Jesus says about worldview because Jesus is setting our common worldviews on their heads. He is giving us a different story line for the understanding of what reality means. This change of story lines, this switch of plots, is at the foundation of all true conversions and, therefore, of all genuine reconstruction.

Getting in Touch With Your Worldview

It will probably not be easy for you to name your operative worldview objectively. It's the grid of your deepest experience.

Your operative worldview is not largely the product of rational or deliberate choice. You absorb it from your parents, from your first years of life and from your formative years in general. In some cases it is altered by a deeply influential person, book or experience.

It's true that even the most enlightened people see their world from a certain defined cultural perspective. But they also see beyond their own biases to something transcendent, something that crosses the boundaries of culture and individual experience. People with a distorted image of self or world or God will be largely incapable of experiencing what is really real in our world. They will see things through a narrow keyhole. They'll see instead what they need reality to be, what they're afraid it is, what they're angry for its being. They'll see everything through their anger, through their fear or agenda. In other words, they won't see *it* at all.

That's the opposite of the contemplative who sees what is, whether it's favorable or not, whether it meets his needs or not, whether she likes it or not, and whether or not it's wept over or rejoiced in. Most of us will usually misinterpret our experience until we have been moved out of our false center. There is too much of the self in the way. Most people do not see things as they are, they see things as *they are*. That is no small point.

Dennis, Sheila and Matthew Linn have written a beautiful book called *Good Goats* (Paulist Press, 1994) that helps us see how many people are trapped by counterproductive and even destructive images of God. When you touch your deepest image of self, a deeper image of reality, or a new truth about God, you're touching something that opens you to the sacred. You'll want to weep or you'll want to be silent, or you'll want to run away from it and change the subject because it's too deep, it's too heavy. As T. S. Eliot says in *Four Quartets*, "human kind cannot bear very much reality" ("Burnt Norton," I).

When we tamper with these images we are changing our own compass and the coordinates of our reality. That's what the Catholic Church dared to do at the Second Vatican Council. In a major way the Council told Roman Catholics of the twentieth century to renew our images of God, of worship and of the very nature of Catholicism, and to return to a much more scripturally based foundation.

After every Council since the beginning of the Church there has been a major schism, a major split, except after Vatican II. We feel we're horribly split into liberals and conservatives, but no formal schism has taken place. The problem now is that I don't think this generation can handle much more psychic change. I don't think it can handle any more liberal changes that will redefine established patterns, at least in this generation. When the psyche is in such a state of disarray and confusion as it is today, it longs for and desperately needs some givens, some absolutes. Again to quote T. S. Eliot, it needs "a still point of the turning world."

That's why my colleagues and I emphasize contemplation. It's the way of going to the experience of the absolute without going toward ideology. Do you see the difference? It's going toward the experience of the good and the true and the beautiful without going into a head trip, or taking the small self too seriously, or taking one's momentary vantage point too seriously either:

> Neither from nor towards; at the still point, there the dance is....
> Where past and future are gathered. Neither movement from
>   nor towards,
> Neither ascent nor decline. Except for the point, the still point,
> There would be no dance, and there is only the dance.
> (T. S. Eliot, "Burnt Norton," II)

Worldview as Matrix of God-image, Self-image, World-image

The God-image, the self-image and the world-image are deeply connected. Normally when one of them changes, the other two have to readjust. So when your God-image changes then *you* have to change. When your world-image is adjusted, you are confused or even depressed for awhile. That's why theology and philosophy were called the king and queen of sciences. In a classic university, all students had to examine these areas or it was not a *uni*-versity (with one center).

For example, if your God is a judge then you'll remain a fearful little girl. And if suddenly God is love you have to learn how to be in love. You have to change. You become the God you worship, as so many have said. You can pretty much assess what a person is like and tell them what their God is like. If they're fear-filled you know what their God-image is.

Another example is easy to find today: practical agnosticism. Unlike atheism, which denies God, it simply says, "I don't know and I don't care." Yet that, too, is an organizing principle. If "I don't know and I don't care" is your "centralizing image," boundaries soon evaporate. There's nothing really demanded, nothing really expected, nothing really needed, nothing really called forth. We just sort of move wherever the ego leads us. Finally, agnosticism amounts to a disorganizing principle rather than organizing anything.

We can see from these examples that when one image changes the others will change as well. If you want to grow in these areas, try to bring your honestly operative images of self and God to conscious consideration. It might even be good to write a journal about this over a period of time. Avoid the temptation to be fashionable or socially acceptable, like saying merely, "My God is love." Don't write it down till it is a felt experience. Let's be honest.

There are a lot of us who are still operating on inadequate or even toxic images of God we learned as children. For example, we're afraid we're going to be shamed, because our early experience of religion was largely God as policeman. Yet, your image of God will improve as you learn more about God. If it is really God you are meeting, it will *only* get better. Take that as absolute.

Attachment to Self-image

Let me give you some possible images of self to examine—always remembering that you have to have a self-image, and it is best to have a positive but honest one, but the only real problem is your *attachment* to it. That is what may become a kind of chosen blindness.

In general, look for both an adjective and a noun in these attempts at a personal self-description: realistic intellectual, ineffective dreamer, convinced Christian, hardworking mother, for example. Be careful when the terms are too positive or too grandiose, because they usually come from what is admired outside rather than what you really are or even want to be. Be careful when they're too negative because you have to live down to them. Yet that might be exactly what you are doing: "living up to" or "living down in," instead of living who you are in God.

Let's say you think of yourself as a positive homemaker. This self-image says, "I'm always positive, I'm always upbeat and always optimistic." That's fine, there's no good or bad to any of these. But if you are too attached to it, you lock yourself into a self-image and then see everything through a distorted lens. You will not be able to see when you are *not* this way, although almost everyone else will! Now one way to tell if you've gone too far is to consider what offends you. If you are hurt when other people do not respond immediately to your cheery housecleaning, then perhaps you've over-identified with the homemaker image. If you are threatened by women who do housekeeping differently, you are too invested in your own nest. Is this not many of the people we all know?

Who-we-are-in-God or "love" takes no offense (1 Corinthians 13:5). The True Self is an indestructible image, as opposed to the "heap of broken images" that Eliot calls the modern "Wasteland." An honest self-image needs neither to be asserted nor defended. It just is, and it is enough. Thus the saints speak of "resting" in God. Only the True Self can rest. The false self is inherently restless.

Some other common self-images include: unhappy child, strong leader, enlightened feminist, poor student, organized manager, gregarious friend. None of these are bad or good. The only problem is your attachment to them.

Look especially for images of dominance or submission in role, intelligence, age, race, class, gender, family of origin. Too much one-sidedness in either direction is usually an indication of the false self. What is it that holds you fast? What's your trap? What is it you have to live up to? That's your enslaving self-image. The saint needs neither to dominate nor to grovel, but can do either one if it is rightly called for. The holy person is thus the ultimately free person. If you *need* to dominate, you are not free not to dominate, and that is not freedom for you or anybody else.

In the spiritual journey you will naturally detach from self-images as you draw closer to God. In God's presence you don't need to stand on your self-image or project your self-image. In truth your overly clad self is what keeps you from God and from other people, because only naked people can make love. To be present with God you will gradually become very transparent and vulnerable, you will gradually let go of roles, titles, masks, identities. They are all in the way. God's perfect loving of you makes it possible to shed your "character armor" (à la Ernest Becker), just as with a true friend. I suspect this is the archetypal fascination of lovers' undressing one another and undressing themselves for the other. That's very powerful stuff, and not just titillation.

If I'm overly self-identified as a realistic intellectual, then God has to come as the realistic intellectual, because that's who I am. He can't come as the humble little man on welfare and speak to me because I can't hear him. If I am over-identified as moral and law abiding, I wonder how one would ever meet the God of mercy and forgiveness, which seems to be God's very name. When God always has to come in our preferred form, then we are in charge, and God is no longer God. Or we will meet a very small part of God.

One of the great graces of growing older is that people often start to let go of spurious and self-serving images. Perhaps the reason for a mid-life crisis is that God is trying to help you let go of your attachment to being a doctor, a priest, a mother or whatever you think you are. Part of the great conversion experience is precisely the ecstatic recognition that "I am not who I *think* I am." It can be a very terrifying thing, even though it is the ultimate liberation. If you have entirely identified with one persona in your 20's, 30's and 40's, you just can't image what you would be without it—which is exactly the problem.

The spiritual life is always about letting go of unnecessary baggage so that we're prepared for death's final letting go. That can only happen if we're willing to know that our self-image is not the deepest me. It's an important and good part of the journey and it might even have helped us to taste moments of the I Am. But there's much more. Finally, like the great Paul, "it is no longer I, but Christ living in me" (Galatians 2:20). My deepest me is God.

Growing Image of World/Reality

Our operative world-image is finally our "realm," that which is real for us and becomes the organizing principle that situates our daily decisions, lifetime choices and ultimate sense of direction and significance. It tends to grow, but also is founded in very early and largely non-rational teachings "at our mother's knee" and our father's example. I knew that the world could be trusted, for example, by the time I was in kindergarten. At least that is when I first remember thinking that way. Probably I "knew" it by three, because I could trust both Mom and Dad.

How do you really see the world? Thomas Jefferson and George Washington, like most of the founding fathers of our country, were deists, sort of like those theists we talked about earlier. They weren't Christian in the real sense of Christian. Deists believe that the universe is like a clock wound up by God and left ticking along without God's further intervention. For the deist, "God is in his heaven and all is right with the world." Certainly God has no active caring or providential guidance for this world. Just an inner kind of logic is unfolding, and he is watching it. If God does step in, it is probably just to punish, which sounds much like the emotionally unavailable father that most people seem to have had in history. Many Americans who go to church regularly are still deists in every practical sense.

Another image of world includes power and struggle as the bottom line. We used to hear the world described as a "veil of tears," an obstacle course, a bunch of hoops for us to jump through. Reality is basically oppositional, testy, antagonistic. Many ancient peoples, especially before the person of Jesus, saw the world as a heroic contest. Just read Germanic and Viking myths, and those of many peoples from harsh climates. It's very understandable: Their physical world naturally became their world-image. One seldom finds such harsh and dour world-images among Polynesian islanders or Sicilian fishermen.

Then there's the perspective that everything's planned, that there's no freedom to God or to the self, that we're just puppets. Everywhere here is the language of fate, karma, destiny and the eternal plan of God. Fundamentalist language sounds like that very often, without much room for God to break *our interpretation* of God's own rules! Yet the biblical tradition had a strong, daring sense of free will, acknowledging both the freedom of God and the freedom of the self. We would do well not to lose that sense of freedom. From an utterly free God come the central mysteries of forgiveness, mercy, providence and election—which by definition are God breaking God's own rules, and always in our favor. How wonderful!

How about the world as survival of the fittest? Or life is just a bowl of cherries? Or the view summed up in the terrible bumper sticker, "Life's a bitch and then you die." Now why would people sport such a bumper sticker unless part of them believes it? They had best be aware of the glasses they wear. *How* you see is *what* you will see.

In looking at your world-image, look especially for any hints of purpose or direction, meaning or plan, or lack of it. Sit alone in the silence today and say, "What do I expect of life? What do I owe life? What does the world offer me? What do I offer the world?" That will pretty much reveal your operative world-image. Is the universe for you or against you? Is it a hostile universe or are there angels in every tree?

CHAPTER NINE

The Great Chain of Being

Francis called all creatures, no matter how small, by the name of brother and sister, because he knew they had the same source as himself.

—Saint Bonaventure, *Major Life, Omnibus*

I WOULD LIKE to reclaim an ancient, evolving and very Franciscan metaphor to rightly name the nature of the universe, God, and the self and to direct our future thinking: the image of the Great Chain of Being.

By this image the Scholastic theologians tried to communicate a linked and coherent world (see *The Great Chain of Being,* Arthur Lovejoy, Harvard University Press, 1936). The essential and unbreakable links in the chain include the Divine Creator, the angelic heavenly, the human, the animal, the world of plants and vegetation, and planet Earth itself with its minerals and waters. In themselves, and in their union together, they proclaim the glory of God (Psalm 104) and the inherent dignity of all things. This image became the basis for calling anything and everything sacred.

What some now call creation spirituality, deep ecology or holistic gospel actually found a much earlier voice in the spirituality of the ancient Celts, the Rhineland mystics and most especially Saint Francis of Assisi. Women like Hildegard of Bingen (1098-1179) communicated it through music, art, poetry and community life itself. Scholars like Saint Bonaventure (1217-1274) created an entire *Summa Theologica* based on Saint Francis' spiritual seeing: "In the soul's journey to God we must present to ourselves *the whole material world* as the first mirror through which we may pass over to the Supreme (Artisan)" *(The Soul's Journey to God,* I, 9. Emphasis added.). The Dominican Meister Eckhart (1260-1327) said the same: "If humankind could have known God without the world, God would never have created the world."

The "Catholic synthesis" of the early Middle Ages was exactly that—a synthesis that held together, for us, one coherent world, a positive intellectual vision not defined by "againstness" or enemies, but by "the clarity and beauty of form." It was a cosmic egg of meaning, a vision of Creator and a multitude of creatures that excluded nothing. The Great Chain of Being was the first holistic metaphor for the new seeing offered us by the Incarnation: Jesus as the living icon of integration, "the coincidence of opposites" who "holds all things in unity" within himself (Colossians 1:15-20). God is One. I am whole and so is everything else.

Sadly we seldom saw the Catholic synthesis move beyond philosophers' books and mystics' prayers. The rest of us Catholics often remained in a fragmented and dualistic world, usually looking for the contaminating element to punish or the unworthy member to expel. While still daring to worship the cosmic Scapegoat—Jesus—we scapegoated the other links in the Great Chain of Being. We have been unwilling to see the Divine Image in those we judge to be inferior or unworthy: sinners, heretics, animals, things growing from Earth and Earth itself. Once the Great Chain of Being was broken, we were soon unable to see the Divine Image in our own species, except for folks just like us. Then it was only a short time before the Enlightenment and modern secularism denied the whole heavenly sphere—unknown in any culture except the recent West—and finally the Divinity itself!

As the medievals predicted, once the chain was broken, and one link not honored, the whole vision collapsed. Either we acknowledge that God is in all things or we have lost the basis for seeing God in anything. Once the choice is ours and not God's, it is merely a world of private preferences and prejudices. The cosmic egg is shattered. I am grateful that the positive formulation persisted in the Franciscan motto and coat of arms: *Deus Meus et Omnia* ("My God and All Things").

Saint Bonaventure, who is called the second founder of the Franciscan Order, took Francis' intuitive genius and spelled it out into an entire philosophy. "The magnitude *of* things...clearly manifests...the wisdom and goodness of the triune God, who by power, presence and essence exists uncircumscribed in all things" *(The Soul's Journey to God,* 1, 14). God is "within all things but not enclosed; outside all things, but not excluded; above all things, but not aloof; below all things, but not debased" (5, 8). Bonaventure was the first to speak of God as one "whose center is everywhere and whose circumference is nowhere" (8). Therefore the origin, magnitude, multitude, beauty, fullness, activity and order of all created things are the very "footprints" and "fingerprints" *(vestigia)* of God. Now that is quite a lovely and very safe universe to live in. Welcome home!

> Whoever, therefore, is not enlightened by such splendor of cre-ated things is blind; whoever is not awakened by such outcries is deaf; whoever does not praise God because of all these effects is dumb; whoever does not discover the First Principle from such clear signs is a fool.
>
> Therefore, open your eyes, alert the ears of your spirit, open your lips and apply your heart so that in all creatures you may see, hear, praise, love and worship, glorify and honor your God, lest the whole world rise against you. (1, 15)

It is hard to imagine how different the last seven hundred years might have been if this truly catholic vision had formed more Christians. But instead, as Bonaventure feared, "The whole world has now risen (in judgment) against" us. Our seeing has been very partial and usually prejudicial, and often not seeing at all. The individual has always decided and discriminated as to where and if God's image would be honored. Sinners, heretics, witches, Moslems, Jews, Indians, native spiritualities, buffalo and elephants, land and water were the losers. And we dared to call ourselves monotheists ("one God" tends to move a people toward one world) or "Christ-like." The Divine Indwelling, subject to our whimsical seeing, seems to dwell nowhere except in temples of our choosing: It seems we have always had a "pro-choice movement."

Until we weep over these sins and publicly own our complicity in the destruction of God's creation, we are surely doomed to remain blind. Pope John Paul II reminded us during the Jubilee preparations and in his dramatic pilgrimages of 2000 that this public repentance is necessary. If not, we will likely keep looking for "acceptable" scape-goats. Journalists, politicians, lawyers and the new restorationists in the Church are fervently hunting for sinners these days, and this in what many claim is a largely secular society. We always think the problem is *elsewhere*, whereas the gospel keeps the pressure of conversion on *me*. As far as the soul is concerned, *no one else is your problem. You are your problem.* You be converted, and live, says the biblical tradition (see Deuteronomy 30:15-20; Mark 1:15).

Jesus tried desperately to keep us within and connected to the Great Chain of Being by taking away from us the power to scapegoat and project onto enemies and outsiders: We were to keep the chain unbroken by not hating, eliminating or expelling the other. He commanded us to love the

enemy and gave us himself as Cosmic Victim so we would get the point—
and stop creating victims. But we are transformed into Christ slowly.

Our inclination to break the chain—to decide who is good and who
is bad—seems to be a basic control mechanism in all of us. We actually
are a bit worried about the God that Jesus believes in: who "causes his
sun to rise on the bad as well as the good, who sends down rain to fall
on the upright and the wicked alike" (Matthew 5:45). If we dishonor the
so-called inferior or unworthy members of creation, we finally destroy
ourselves, too. Once we stop seeing, we stop seeing. Like nothing else,
spiritual transformation is an all-or-nothing proposition. Like Jesus'
robe, it is a "seamless garment." He wore it and offers it to us.

Saint Paul did for Jesus exactly what Saint Bonaventure did for
Francis. He took the life lived and made it into a philosophy/theology.
The seamless garment is still intact in Paul's most-quoted analogy of
the body:

> If one part is hurt, all parts are hurt with it. If one part is given
> special honor, all parts enjoy it...[and] it is precisely the parts of
> the body that seem to be the weakest which are the indispensable
> ones, and it is the least honorable parts of the body that we clothe
> with the greatest care. (1 Corinthians 12:26, 22-23)

Paul, the former mass-murderer Saul, knew well religion's power to
create hate and violence toward other people and other links in the
Great Chain of Being. He left no room for scapegoating in his teaching:
There is "one God and [Creator] of all, over all, through all and within
all" (Ephesians 4:6, NJB).

For those given sight by the gospel, there is only one world—God's
world—and it is *all* supernatural! We may no longer divide the world
into sacred and profane (*fanum* and *profanum*). There is cosmic sym-
bolism in the tearing of the Temple veil from top to bottom at the death
of Jesus (Matthew 27:51). In the one world liberated by Christ, our
need to divide and discriminate has been denied us—and frankly, we
don't like it. For some reason, we want to retain the right to decide
where God is, whom we must honor and whom we may hate. It's a
rather clever guise, for I can remain autonomous and violent while
thinking of myself as holy. But, as Jesus reminds us, any branch cut off
from the vine is useless (John 15:5-6). We either go to God *linked* or it
seems we don't go at all.

How easy it is to avoid the seating and sacramental mystery:
"Listen, Israel, the Lord your God is One" (Deuteronomy 6:4). Jewish
monotheism became the basis for one coherent and cosmic world,

where truth is one and there is no basis for rivalry between the arts, science and religion. If it is true it is true, regardless of its source. It is such truth that will set us free (John 8:32).

In his brilliant contemporary synthesis, *A Brief History of Everything* (Shambhala Publications, 1996), Ken Wilber sounds like a postmodern Thomas Aquinas or Bonaventure. He concludes that "everything is a *holon*." A *holon* is defined as something that is simultaneously whole within itself and yet also part of something larger. He explains the concept at length in *Sex, Ecology, Spirituality* (Shambhala, 1995) that everything in the physical, biological, psychic and spiritual universe is a whole and yet a part. Ours really is *one* connected universe of meaning. And in relation to the arrogance of modernism and the cynicism of postmodernism, Wilber only adds, "No epoch is finally privileged. We are all tomorrow's food." Agreeing with the genuinely *traditional* Catholic, he reminds us that even our moment in time is a *holon*, a small chain-link in something still larger.

A Great Catholic—one who embraces the whole Tradition—would call this one connected universe the Cosmic Christ, before whom no institution, no moment of time, no attempt at verbalization will be adequate. We must hold the hands of both ancestors and children, and hold them well.

Those who continue to look through microscopes and telescopes are surrendering to the mysteries of an infinite, creative spectrum. The chain of being is even longer and bigger than we church folks imagined—and we had best come to the telescope and microscope with our shoes off and ready to live the emptiness of not knowing. Maybe we are just beginning to see how broad the "communion of saints" might be—and whether we really want to believe in it.

CHAPTER TEN

The Power of Forgiveness

· · · · · · · · · · · · · ·

YOU COULD SAY that among the most powerful of human experiences is to give or to receive forgiveness. I am told that two-thirds of the teaching of Jesus is directly or indirectly about this mystery of forgiveness, God's breaking of God's own rules. That's not surprising, because forgiveness is probably the only human action that *reveals three goodnesses simultaneously!* When we forgive, we choose the goodness of the other over their faults, we experience God's goodness flowing through ourselves and we also experience our own goodness in a way that almost surprises us. That is an awesome coming together of power, both human and divine.

I want to share with you a personal story of forgiveness that happened in my family near the time of my mother's death. I was supposed to travel home, back to Kansas, thinking my mother would already be gone by then and we'd have the funeral. We had spent many good visits together during her final days and she seemed ready to go. After hearing that she was hanging on, I delayed my trip for a few days. I didn't expect what happened when I got there.

I was sitting by the bed of my mother and I told her how I'd miss her. Now, as I have described before, this earthy, farming woman was no sentimentalist. All of a sudden she said to me, "I want to hear it from him." And I said, "What?"

She: "Him."

I: "You mean Daddy?"

She: "Yeah, I want to hear if he's going to miss me."

So I ran over to my father, at that point a man of eighty-four, whom we still call "Daddy." For weeks, months he had been telling her that he would miss her, but she wanted to hear it one more time from him. So I said, "Daddy, she wants to hear that you're going to miss her." He came over and effusively told her, "Oh, I'm gonna miss ya."

She replied, "I don't believe it."

I couldn't believe my ears! I said, "Mother, you're a few hours from death. You can't say that!"

She persisted: "I don't believe it."

Daddy redoubled his efforts: "I ask your forgiveness for all the times I've hurt you in our fifty-four years of marriage and I forgive you for the times you've hurt me." I said, "Mother, isn't that beautiful. Now, say that back to Daddy." And suddenly she clammed up. She didn't want to say it. (Typical Enneagram eight!)

I never felt more the priest. Here I had to coach my own mother. I said, "Mother, you're soon going to be before God. You don't want to come before God without forgiving everybody."

She said, "I forgive everybody."

I said, "But do you forgive Daddy?" and she became silent again.

Then Daddy jumps in he says, "Honey, I never fooled around with any other women."

We all knew that. She even said, "Well I know that, I know that."

My siblings and I still don't know what the big thing was. But any married person knows there are many little ways a couple hurt one another over fifty-four years. There are little grudges, perhaps even big ones, which you hold. So I told her, "Mother you know the Our Father. You're only going to get as much forgiveness from God as you've given. Now, you've got to forgive Daddy."

She kept her eyes closed. I pulled every Christian trick out of the bag, but she kept her eyes closed. Nothing was working.

Then I said, "Mother, let's try this, I'm going to put one hand on your heart and I'm going to pray that your heart gets real soft." I held her other hand and I started kissing it while I held the other hand over her heart.

After about a minute she said, very faintly, "That melts me."

I: "What?"

She: "When you kiss my hand like that, now I've got to do it."

After a pause she continued: "I'm a stubborn woman, all my life I've been a stubborn woman."

"Well, Mother, we all knew that," I said. "Now look at Daddy and you tell him."

So she looked over and she didn't say "Daddy," as she usually did. She spoke to him by name: "Rich, I forgive you." (His name was Richard, too.)

I prompt her again: "Mother, the other half—I ask for your forgiveness."

She started breathing really quick, breathing so heavily I thought it was the end. Then she summoned her energy. She said, "Rich, I ask your forgiveness." She continued with the heavy breathing. And she said, "That's it, that's it. That's what I had to do."

She had been talking for days during the previous week about "a mesh." I couldn't understand what it was. She had said, "There's a mesh that I'm trying to get through." Now I said to her, "Mother, do you think that was the mesh?" She replied, "It's gone! The mesh is gone! And, God, I pray that I mean this forgiveness from my heart." This was only four days before she died.

Now that might seem like a tiny thing, but that's the way that we can be clogged up, the way we can be blocked. Then she said, referring to my two sisters and my sisters-in-law, "Tell the girls to do this early and not to wait 'til now. They'll understand a woman's heart and the way a man can hurt a woman."

I'm not sure, but I think all of this might have come from an old quarrel over something most of us would consider insignificant. But as married people know, some of those struggles carry a deeper symbolic meaning in the relationship. All we knew was that Daddy occasionally ran over her flowers with the lawnmower! She claimed it was intentional, and we ourselves sometimes wondered. He was the grass man and she was the flower woman, and they both fought for more space. I suppose it was a symbol of something much deeper in their souls—not hard to figure out, and on that level little things can, in fact, be quite deep and significant. Symbols perhaps, but symbolic action is often the real action, especially it seems to many women.

Whatever it had been about, I was utterly happy. I said, "Aren't you glad you said it, Mother?" She said, "I'm so happy, I'm so happy." My sister came in a few minutes later and before I had a chance to tell her the conversation, she had talked to mother and then she came running back to me. She said, "Mother says the mesh is gone and that she's so happy."

That's the power and the grace of forgiveness. In my own life, and with my own stalwart mother.

But let's do it *now* and not wait until later! Let's ask for the grace to let go of those grudges and those hurts that we hold onto. How else will we ever be free? Let's live inside of that wonderful good news that says with Saint Catherine of Genoa, "My deepest me is God!" We have come forth from God, we are sons and daughters and heirs of something that we did not create. In forgiveness we live up to our truest dignity, we operate by a power not our own. We live out of the True Self and not just the tiny self that is always offended and complaining. This is the genuinely new thing that true believers have to offer the world.

We Are 'Like' God

David Tracy, one of the best theologians on the American scene, wrote a book called *The Analogical Imagination* (Crossroad, 1985). With great scholarship he concludes that "the great Catholics," who've really been transformed by their catholic worldview, have an "analogical" way of seeing reality. They see God and their own reality as analogous, or "like." It is the result of the Catholic/Christian emphasis on Incarnation, I believe. It always sees heaven and earth as mirroring each another, not distinct, but in fact most similar. "As above, so below," we would say; or if you argue from the other side, "As below, so above." In either case you have a wonderfully coherent and sacramental universe.

The Catholic mind, at least in its heyday, represented "the analogical imagination." It was always emphasizing, "God is like..., God is similar..., We are image of..., God is the same as..." (Saint Bonaventure's "*vestigia Dei*," from the previous chapter, the very fingerprints of God). All the world is a poem about God; all of reality is an analogy for God. And this, of course, had a good side and a bad side. The good side was you could be at home in the real world. The "actual" was the place of grace, not the idealized or "religious" world.

You'll still see this in Mediterranean Catholic countries, where the Catholic imagination took the strongest hold on culture. They don't apologize for fiestas and holidays, for drinking, eating, sex and dancing. That was still a bit shadowy to the Nordic Catholics, the Teutonic and Anglo-Saxon types—they never really got the humorous, ironic side of human existence, so well summarized in the jingle, "Wherever the Catholic sun does shine, there is singing and dancing and good red wine. At least the Bible tells me so, *Benedicamus Domino*." Ironically, this was written by an English Catholic, Hilaire Belloc.

David Tracy claimed that, in general, the Protestant mind, and the Jewish mind, too, imagine things differently. They tend to emphasize *the difference* between God and the world. In the Protestant case, you can see it in the theology of Karl Barth and many of the Swiss reformers, who continuously emphasize the "otherness of God." You certainly see that same emphasis on transcendence in much Jewish spirituality, too: "Holy, Holy, Holy, Lord God of Hosts." The Incarnation would be unthinkable to the normal Jew, which is why it is still so strange that it happened there! As always, we both have part of the truth. God is both immanent (present in the world) and transcendent (beyond ordinary experience) in good theology, it seems to me. We Catholics emphasized the immanence for good and for ill; Protestants and Jews, and Moslems too, emphasized transcendence for good and for ill.

The bad side was that Catholicism tended to get pretty slack. God was almost too chummy and forgiving. That's what our Protestant brothers and sisters rightly challenged us on. At one point, two-thirds of the year was feast days and holidays in Italy. Talk about the opposite of the Protestant work ethic! All they did was party! Life meant being at home in this world with God and one another, and our bodies. The Catholic comfort with drinking is still scandalous to many of our Protestant brothers and sisters. But Catholic countries are also notorious for tolerating dictators, political corruption, bribes, greedy upper classes and non-democratic/non-accountable leadership. Our political record is put to shame by clear-headed Anglo-Saxon and Protestant respect for law and accountability. God at a distance and God as policeman does have its social merits.

There has always been a kind of cultural Catholicism which doesn't really take the Gospels seriously (we did not even read them!), or take Jesus' teaching very seriously (we preferred saccharine Sacred Heart novenas), yet at the same time it often produced very compassionate and forgiving people. It retained a kind of mysticism that was lost elsewhere. Protestantism always seemed to produce people who were filled with judgments and criticisms of everything, yet it also produced people much more submitted to the concrete teaching of Jesus and much more socially responsible, in my opinion: the Mennonites on simple living; the Quakers on war; the Lutherans on grace; the Pentecostals on the Holy Spirit; the Amish, Congregationalists and Presbyterians on different aspects of practical community; the Holiness Churches on sheer joy in God.

The analogical imagination at its best creates very patient and less judgmental people. I think they feel less judged by God and tend to be more tolerant of others. It's "forgive us as we forgive them" kind of thinking. Perhaps it's nowhere better symbolized in literature than Graham Greene's *The Power and the Glory*. Greene was a great Catholic in his imaginal world, as were Walker Percy, Victor Hugo, François Mauriac and Flannery O'Connor. They lived and wrote out of the analogical imagination. Perhaps you remember the hero of Greene's novel, "the whiskey priest," the drunk! But Greene makes him dear, a saint, an everyman. "He could still put God on men's tongues": That was the shocking idea. God uses sinners, which is all of us. The whiskey priest was still the mediator between God and humanity, drunk or not. The people still kissed his hand knowing his sin, but knowing that God forgives all sin, that we all are sinners. A sincere Protestant could never have written that book. The sinner is too unlike God to ever be used by God or set up as any kind of hero.

If you don't get forgiveness, you're missing the whole mystery. You are still living in a world of meritocracy, of quid-pro-quo thinking, a world of performance and behavior that earns an award. Forgiveness is the great thawing of all logic and reason and worthiness. It is a melting into the mystery of God as unearned love, unmerited grace, the humility and powerlessness of a Divine Lover. Forgiveness is the beginning, the middle and the end of the whole gospel, as far as I can see.

Without radical and rule-breaking forgiveness—received and given—there will be no reconstruction of anything. It alone breaks down our damnable world of trying to buy and sell grace. Grace is certainly the one gift that must always be free, perfectly free—to work. Without forgiveness there will be no future. We have hurt one another in too many historically documented and remembered ways. The only way out of the present justified hatreds of the world is grace.

What Is Behind Hate?

Hate, though, which we looked at in Chapter Two, is unfortunately here to stay. Hate can be helpful to certain causes. It unites a group quickly, it gives a person identity even if it is a negative one, and most of all it takes away doubt and all free-floating anxiety. It gives us a place to stand that feels superior and in control. Hate settles the dust and ambiguity that none of us like. Hate is much more common, and more immediately effective than love. Hate, as we will sadly see below, makes the world go 'round.

You could say, in fact, that Jesus came to resolve the central and essential problem of hate. There is no other way to save us from ourselves, to save us from one another and therefore to "save us" unless we are saved from our need to hate. We have produced so much utopian talk about Jesus and love, but Jesus had a very hard time getting to the issue of love. First he had to expose and destroy the phenomenon of hate. Once he exposed the lie and illusion of hate, love could show itself clearly—and it did.

The pattern is still unfortunately the same. As Jesus shockingly put it, "Satan is the real prince of this world" (John 12:31). Hate, it seems, is the ordinary, daily agenda. Love is the totally enlightened, entirely nonsensical way *out* of the ordinary agenda. The gospel presents the dilemma in a personal and cathartic narrative that grounds the whole issue in history and in one man's enlightened response to our history. One man, Jesus, accepts the religious and social judgment of hate and bears the consequences publicly, but in an utterly new way that transforms the pattern and the possibilities. For two thousand years, he has remained the most striking icon of a possible new agenda. His death exposed the lie and the problem like never before. His risen life tells people their lives could have a different story line. He did not just give us textbook answers from a distance, but personally walked through the process and said, "Follow me."

I believe that fear is almost always behind hate. Sometimes it looks like control, but even control freaks are usually afraid of losing something. It is almost always fear that justifies hatred, but a fear that is hardly ever recognized as such. "The angels of darkness must always disguise themselves as angels of light" (2 Corinthians 11:14). The best and most convincing disguise for fear is virtue itself, or godliness. Then it never looks like fear.

For fear to survive, it must look like reason, prudence, commonsense, intelligence, the need for social order, morality, religion, obedience, justice or even spirituality. It always works. What better way to veil vengeance than to call it justice? What better way to cover greed than to call it responsible stewardship? Only people who have moved beyond ego and controlling of all outcomes, only those practiced at letting go, see fear for the impostor that it is. To be trapped inside of your small ego is always to be afraid.

To not have anyone that you can trust is necessarily to be a control freak. Thus great religion tries its best to free individuals from the tyranny of their small and fragile selves. It always points toward a larger identity that we call the Godself, the True Self, the self "hidden with Christ in God" (Colossians 3:3), the trustworthy Lover. Healthy and true religion, like Jesus himself, tells you that there is Someone you *can* trust. You do not have to create all the patterns, and you do not have to fix all the failures. What else would be the beginnings of peace?

If the small ego is not transformed, one other pattern is inevitable. The fear is too destabilizing and unsettling for the small self to bear alone, and it must either be denied or projected elsewhere. The process of both denying *and* projecting your fears and hatreds is called "scapegoating," discussed in Chapter Two, from the Jewish ritual of putting your faults on a goat that was whipped out into the desert (see Leviticus 16). The object of our wrath, like the poor "escaping goat," is completely arbitrary and artificial. It has nothing to do with truth or reason. It has to do with fear. Then a plausible and much needed projection screen will always be found for our little drama.

The amazing thing is how well it works. We rather easily displace our fears onto other people, other issues, other places and other times. Anything seems better to us than bearing the burden of my-fear-here-now-myself. Only the Great Self can carry such anxiety, such ambiguity, such essential insecurity. It is much too much for the small self to carry.

So we are stuck with ever new brands of hate. Some have said that the best we have been able to do in the last forty years is to move hatred to ever higher forms of sophistication and ever more subtle forms of disguise. But we still love to hate: Feminists can hate men, liberals can hate conservatives, activists can hate rich people, good family values folks can hate homosexuals and victims can hate perpetrators. We just change the vocabulary to make it sound well thought out. This twice-distilled hate is now legitimate, necessary, deserved and very well disguised! Jesus would call it "driving out the devil by the prince of devils," hating supposed evil and becoming hatred ourselves—but now even better hidden from ourselves and difficult to expose. Now we hate under the banner of God and goodness and political correctness. This is the prince of devils, for sure, a devil almost impossible to drive out.

Paul the Pharisee had to be thrown to the ground and the scales had to painfully fall from his eyes for him to recognize that in the name of his religion he had become hate, and even mass-murderer. The cock had to crow several times before the first pope, Peter, could recognize that he was doing the very thing he said he would *never* do. Yet these are the two figures that stand in front of the largest church in Christendom as the two pillars of the Roman Church. They were not saints by later, pious definitions, but instead they were transformed examples of hatred and fear. This is not the rare exception, this is the norm and pattern.

It seems there is something we know by losing and finding that we never would have known by simply being safe and sweet. The greatest lovers are not uncommonly the same people who once hated and feared. Virtue is not just will power, but actually vice overcome.

Both René Gírard and Gil Bailie have taught us that the most effective and common way to turn social hatred into social harmony is via a scapegoat. It works so well, it gathers the community so quickly, that it has perdured through most of human history. Now it is the normal story line, so normal that we hardly see it. It remains denied, invisible and unaware.

'Sacred' Violence

Carl Jung saw the same pattern in the individual that Gírard sees in society and culture: That which you fear, deny and avoid will be projected somewhere else with one hundred percent certainty! In other words, there is an intrinsic connection between fear, hatred and violence. Furthermore, you will do it with impunity and even grandiosity. It is the sacralization of violence, and is the most common form of violence. That way we can be hateful and not feel the least guilty about it, but in fact feel morally superior!

The process of sacred violence is so effective that it is now in the "hard wiring" of human personality. As Aquinas said, no one intentionally does evil, they have to explain it to themselves as good! I am sad to say that, historically, religion is the most effective proponent of hatred and fear, and therefore violence.

Sacred violence is the most common kind of violence. How strange that we could ever arrive at this place after Jesus said that he came for "the forgiveness of sin" and the perfect love that casts out all fear! It's no surprise that he has to spend a great part of his ministry in an attempt to reform religion itself. Religion is ironically the safest place to hide from God! In its healthy forms, it is also the place to find God. As the Latin scholars said, "the corruption of the best is always the worst."

We see the classic pattern already in Adam's treatment of Eve, and Cain's killing of Abel. It is the original lie, and continues nonstop until now. It is called history, largely a record of who kills, imprisons, tortures, oppresses, controls, enslaves, rapes, occupies or exploits whom. That's really quite disappointing, once you see it. Then the utterly predictable response is revenge or retribution. The old and only story line continues unabated. It never stops, and at this point is getting quite boring. We need a new plot beyond "get the bad guys."

It is only the mystics and seers in all of the great religions who give us a genuinely new story: redemptive suffering instead of redemptive violence. Socrates, Jesus, the Mother of the Maccabees, Buddha, Harriet Tubman, Gandhi and Oscar Romero—these give us a genuinely new story line. These few are the true history makers, who expose the self-serving lie of hatred and open a way through for the rest of history. The rest are only delaying the resurrection of humanity.

Resurrection will be taken care of for us, as quietly as a silent Sunday morning, once the lie of Friday has been exposed and thereby undercut. Once Jesus put all his effort and energy into Friday, God took care of Sunday easily. But as the Gospel texts say, "suddenly there was a violent earthquake...the guards were...like dead men" (Matthew 28:2, 4). The game of smoke and mirrors was over—for good, but it is a continuing seismic shift to the imperial system.

Love, Infectious and Free

As a Christian, I do believe that Jesus' death was a historical breakthrough, and it is no accident that Christians date history around his life. Afterwards, we could never quite see things in the same way. The "virus" of the gospel was forever released into human history, archetypally pictured as blood flowing from the crucified. It was only a minority of Christians who ever got the point, however. But now the toothpaste cannot be put back into the tube, the movement of grace cannot be reversed.

Most Christians, with utter irony, worshipped Jesus the Scapegoat on Sundays and made scapegoats of Jews, Moslems, other Christian denominations, heretics, sinners, pagans, the poor and almost anybody who was not like them the other six days of the week. One would have thought that Christians who "gazed upon the one they had pierced" would have gotten the message about how wrong domination, power and hatred can be. The system had been utterly wrong about their own, chosen God figure, yet they continued to trust the system. I guess they did not gaze long enough.

Many followers of other religions seem to have been infected by the virus more than many nominal Christians. Girard says that the Christian West was the "most destabilized" by the virus of the gospel, and moved into overdrive to cover its fear and its need to hate, despite the orders from its designated God. The central teaching of Jesus on love of enemies, forgiveness and care for those at the bottom was supposed to make scapegoating virtually impossible and unthinkable.

Scapegoating depends upon a rather sophisticated, but easily learned ability to compartmentalize, to separate, to divide the world into the pure and the impure. Anthropologically all religion begins with the creation of the "impure" and very soon an entire moral system of taboos, punishments, fears, guilts and even a priesthood to enforce it emerges. It gives us a sense of order, control and superiority, which is exactly what the ego wants and the small self demands. And before you start hating the historical religions too much—think about red meat, patriarchy, bourgeois values, all institutions, sexist language and Christianity itself. These have become the new "impure" contaminants.

(Remember, it only gets more sophisticated and justified!)

The absolute religious genius of Jesus is that he utterly refuses all debt codes, purity codes, religious quarantines and the searching for sinners. He refuses the very starting point of historic religion. He refuses to divide the world into the pure and the impure, much to the chagrin of almost everybody—then and now.

Jesus is shockingly *not* upset with sinners, a shock so total that most Christians to this day refuse to see it. He is only upset with people *who do not think* they are sinners: These denying, fearful and illusory ones are the blockage. They are much more likely to hate and feel no compunction. Formerly, religion thought its mission was "to expel sin and evil from River City." After Jesus we find out that sin lies in the very act of expelling. There is no place to expel it to. We have met the enemy, and the enemy is *us*. We either carry and transform the evil of human history as our own problem, or we only increase its efficiency and power by hating and punishing it "over there." The Jesus pattern was put precisely and concisely by Saint Paul: "for our sake he made the sinless one a victim for sin, so that in him we might become the uprightness of God" (2 Corinthians 5:21). I admit, that is heavy stuff. Only the mystics and the sinners seem to get it.

In Jesus' famous story of the Good Samaritan, he has the "man by the side of the road" waking up in enemy territory realizing that he has been loved by the very one who is supposed to hate him and that he is supposed to fear. Could this be everybody's awakening? Could this be an accurate image of God discovery, and truth discovery? He is clearly presenting the foreign Samaritan as a very image of God. He ends the shocking parable by saying, "Go and do the same" (Luke 10:37). The human task has become the very "imitation of God," which seems almost unthinkable. God, the one that history has been taught to fear, is in fact the Utter Goodness that enfolds us and creates a safe and non-threatening universe for us—a renewed universe that we can now pass on to others.

For Jesus there are no postures, group memberships, behaviors, prayer rituals, dietary rules, asceticism or social awareness that of themselves transform us or make us enlightened, saved or superior. There are no contaminating elements or people to expel or exclude. These will be exposed as inadequate when goodness is exposed all the more. If that is not the moral message that shouts from Calvary, I cannot imagine what the message is.

There is no redemptive violence. There is only redemptive suffering. Yes, hate is the norm, but hate is never the future. It is the old and dead story.

CHAPTER ELEVEN

Limits Are Good Teachers

· · · · · · · · · · · · · · · · ·

A WONDERFUL spiritual director from my own hometown in Kansas, Loretta Ross-Gotta, sent me a poem. I would like to begin this chapter with it because it summarizes at the beginning what I am going to belabor with prose. She called it, "In Praise of Boundaries":

Glory be to God for bounds and limits.

Thanks be for fences, for barbed wire, padlocks, bolts, abrupt unmoving dead ends, for stop signs, ramparts, split rails, outlines, outskirts, contours, confines, borders, margins, hedges and rims, shores, banks and brows.

Blessed art thou for shalts and for shalt nots, for oughts and shoulds, for prohibition, inhibition and command.

I praise thee for enclosure, circumference, courtyard, croft, crib, corral and coupe, pen, balustrade, fold, chamber, hutch and manger, paddock, coat, stall, palisade, parapets, trellis, enclave and wall.

So blessed by thee for bindings, wrappings, swaddling clothes, for all quilts, covers, comforters, and counterpane, for lids, roofs, tents, holes, shell and pod, and all that partitions holy from profane.

Thank you kind and gentle God for edges, parameters, and the delicate beauty of borders, thin, that separate this from that.

Yes from no, the skin from the juice, and thou sweet Trinity from me.

Praise and laud forever unto thee oh thou art a most exulted canopy in thy strong shelter sleeps the virgin safe and free.

All creatures great and small be wary. (Loretta Ross-Gotta)

As I have discussed earlier in this book, one of the bad effects of the philosophy of progress is that it allowed a group of people to grow up without a sense of appropriate and necessary limits. In the era of supposedly limitless progress, we've expected far too much of one another. Loretta Ross-Gotta's poem, in lauding appropriate limits, names that for me. There must be beginnings and endings to things, it seems. *Only distinct things can, in fact, make love and create union. And true union ironically differentiates things more than melds them into one.* That is a major and often-confused paradox.

I grew up in the 1960's when we read wonderful books like Josef Goldbrunner's *Holiness Is Wholeness* (Pantheon, 1955). I totally agree with that on one level, but the trouble is that we grew up really expecting things to be whole! What a recipe for disillusionment. We grew up expecting far too much from institutions, from the Church, from one another and, finally, too much from ourselves. We expected the small self to attain the grandeur of God.

Now we have a widespread complaint of young people that they hate themselves. If you really believe that the small self can be whole or if you try to build your self-image on other people's response, you are set up for disaster. The most you will have is momentary rushes of significance, episodic self-esteem that will last you a couple of days. But it cannot be sustained, except by "upping the dosage," which finally becomes the addictive and destructive personality. Or conversely, you will live beneath everyone else's judgments and critiques. It is no surprise that the word *codependent* emerged so strongly in the last decades. Secular people have no other place to live except in a revolving hall of mirrors—which themselves are being mirrored by other mirrors. That's scary. It has created a very fragile kind of person.

Self-esteem comes naturally when I am aligned with who-I-am-in-God. It is inherently unstable when I try to create it out of my own psyche, behavior or fame. The small self on its own, or seeking its significance through the approval of others, will never finally ground us. Because the next day I have to say again: "What do I do today to be important, to be significant, to be thought well of? How can I be famous for more than twenty minutes? Maybe my only choice is infamy?" Often when the positive cannot be attained or sustained, people move toward the negative for cosmic significance: "At least I can get my name in the paper for killing everybody at school or shooting a famous person."

The false self, the small self, the autonomous I, "the branch cut off from the Vine is useless" (John 15:4-5). We had the right idea about being *whole,* but the trouble is that we thought we could do it independ-

ently and within our private personality. That is the eternal lie of the
ego. The ego refuses to admit its own limits and boundaries, and thus
always self-destructs. It either inflates itself by itself (pride), or it
deflates under the awareness of its own insufficiency (self-hatred).

Entitlement Is a Poor Teacher

A sense of limits offers a much more honest attitude about what we can
expect from life. We are set up for anger and judgment when we expect
too much from one another, from the world and from institutions. This
is called a sense of entitlement, and characterizes most people who are
rich, from developed countries, and most younger people born into the
new world of "rights." Our parents and grandparents grew up instead in
a world of responsibility. We are still searching for the happy middle
between those two.

Most people learn a sense of limits much earlier in the Third World.
Observing such people is what gives me the courage to speak this way.
People in the Third World are usually in need and have a right to more,
to justice, but they also have *a much more honest expectation of reality.*
They have a more properly shaped ego. The tragic, the broken, the sinful is already woven into reality. We in the West have gotten away with
a false entitlement that did not weave the tragic into our worldview. We
actually suffer more because of it. Anyone who has been there will tell
you that the poor in the Third World tend to smile more than the middle
class or the wealthy in any country.

Remember, the cross tells us that there is *a cruciform pattern to all
reality,* a collision of cross-purposes, as we discussed in Chapter Two;
our world is filled with contradictions needing to be reconciled, incon-
sistencies within us and between us. Life is neither perfectly consistent
and rational nor is it a chaotic mess. It does contain, however, constant
paradoxes, exceptions and flaws. That is the shocking and disappointing revelation of the cross. It is also a great weight off our backs. It
leads to patience, humility, nonjudgment and suffering love. Now we
have the right sense of proportion, limits, expectations and no room for
utopianism, ideologies, any "final solutions," cynicism or needless discouragement. The shape of things is finally honest and humble. Here
we can live with "faith" (that God is in the contradictions!) instead of
grandiose explanations. Please think about that at great length!

People are talking about this when they talk about simple living.
Simplicity of lifestyle might be, after all, the most radical form of social
justice possible. It is a nonpretentious way of simply living outside of

the whole system of greed, consumption and injustice. Simplicity is clearly going to have to be part of any kind of reconstruction. Any rebuilding must move toward a more modest sense of self. The grandiose self is like a fragile but giant balloon bouncing around a room, and often demanding more inflation to avoid the inevitable. In the postmodern world, people set themselves up to be offended and to be addictive by their false sense of entitlement. Yet the only real enti-tle-ment is from God. When "your name is written in heaven," then all other titles are superfluous and even burdensome.

Ken Keyes says, "so much more suffering comes into the world because of people *taking* offense than from people *giving* offense." We've created a highly offendable people who think they deserve an awful lot—and even have a right to it. The small self has to puff itself up because underneath it knows it is all a sham. A friend of mine who is an airline attendant said that attendants often fight over who has to take the first-class section of the plane. No one wants it, she said. The people are much more fun and more appreciative in economy.

Entitlement is a big theme in Alcoholics Anonymous and AlAnon. Many with alcoholic personalities have lost so much that they feel that the world owes them back. It is a form of narcissism, but it goes beyond the alcoholic personality. Such narcissism has led us to become this highly litigious society where we sue other people when they do not give us what we think we have earned or have a right to. I am told that America has seven times as many lawyers as Japan, and many more than most other countries. We go to the level of court and law and money to achieve what the court and law and money will never be able to give you: self-esteem. Only God can give you your dignity. Maybe that is why Paul told the early Christians never to go to court (1 Corinthians 6:7-8).

'You' Have Never Been Hurt

The True Self can never be hurt, nor has ever been hurt. The only pain it suffers is longing for God and absence from God. It is only the false self that suffers and takes offense, and hopefully those sufferings lead you to collapse back into the True Self. The false self is necessarily insecure and always hurt.

The True Self is indestructible and cannot be offended. The True Self does not stand around waiting for you to like it before it can like itself. It doesn't wait for accolades or external successes before it can believe in itself. It quietly knows.

G. K. Chesterton spoke of the "mystical minimum," which he defined as *gratitude*. When we stand in the immense abundance of the True Self, there is no time or space for being hurt. We are always secure and at rest, and foundationally grateful. Saint Ignatius said that it would take him twenty-five minutes to get over the pain if the pope condemned his Society of Jesus! That is the abundant, grateful Self speaking. The false self does not even understand such silliness.

The grateful response for what is given—seeing the cup half full—requires seeing with a completely different set of eyes than the eyes that always see the cup half empty. I don't think it's oversimplification to say that people basically live either in an attitude of gratitude or an overall attitude of resentment. The mystical minimum is gratitude: Everything that is given, that you are breathing today, is pure gift. None of us have earned it, none of us have a right to it. All we can do is kneel and kiss some ground—somewhere, anywhere, everywhere.

I certainly believe in human rights, and would not want to make light of them, but as such the Bible never talks about "human rights." The only rights the Bible talks about are the rights of widows, orphans and the poor. The little ones have rights that must be respected, and the Word of God always protects the bottom and the unprotected. But in our typical Western narcissism, we use God to protect the top, the elite, those who have too much already. Welfare used to be for the unemployed, now it is for Chrysler and the military! Even the Canon Law of the Church protects the clergy's rights much more than those of the laity or of "the widows and orphans." I am sure you have all seen the excellent poster with the words: "It will be a new world when education is fully funded, and the generals have to have bake sales to buy their bombers."

We wait, it seems, for a shift in consciousness from an exclusive sense of rights and entitlement to consciousness balanced with a sense of responsibility and social obligation. We seem still to be in one swing of the pendulum. When civilization is growing and empowering, it makes use of the language of responsibility: what I, in fact, *owe* to my family, my people, my country, the earth, God. The present ungrateful complaining and blaming will get us nowhere. Now we can "play the victim" and use justice language, or falsely claim, "I am suing only because I don't want this to happen to others" for our own advantage. In fact, it can be the most disguised power trip of all, and just the opposite of how Jesus used his victimhood. He used it to liberate others. We use it to empower ourselves and to punish others.

We do have rights, and most of us thank God for this new insistence on human rights and human dignity, but someone must also protect the rights of the *whole*, the common good. If they do today, they are considered moralistic, or dogmatic or coercive. Here the conservatives are far ahead of most "progressive" thinkers who have made an idol of individuality and personal freedom/license. Someone does have the right to protect society, institutions and groups. If all we have is individual rights, we will tear one another apart in the fray.

I think we have created a mentality that disallows any "calling power" over us. We want to live as if no one is ever going to tell us what we need to do. As if we are the final arbiters of all of our decisions, all of our choices, and we will not allow other persons or institutions—not even a married partner in some cases—to make demands on us. Free choice itself has become our idol. "I choose, therefore I am" has become the new Cartesian formula. Such "freedom" will end up destroying all freedom for everybody, I am afraid. The only way to hold such a society together will be by more and more laws, and enforcement of those laws. And then come the endless prisons to hold those who do not comply, after we idealized "free choice" for them! Restraint and limits are declared a "non-virtue" in our society—except that the poor and the criminally inclined are supposed to practice it! I do not think we can have it both ways.

Virtue is not one isolated value, but a relationship between several values. When personal freedom is isolated from love, temperance, the common good, we have a demon instead of a virtue. True virtue is another name for Sophia or Holy Wisdom. Wisdom is clearly more than mere intelligence, knowledge of facts or information. Virtuous people recognize limits, balance and other people's virtues, too. Wisdom is more synthesis than analysis, more paradoxical than linear, more a dance than a march. Wise people avoid the ideological hysteria that claims, "This is the whole truth, the only truth, the only way to look at it," and too often in the name of some denied but self-serving concern.

When we have a new insight or experience, we tend to absolutize that experience and dismiss everything previous to it. I see a lot of that in America since we are a "now" society. We read a new book, and we temporarily see what we find there as the only way to interpret everything—throwing out the first thirty years of our lives and all other paradigms of explanation. No wonder people are fragmented.

You can usually mistrust any explanation that says "only." At that point you are dealing with idealized, fabricated realities (false religion) and not incarnate and cruciform reality (true religion). It is precisely in this sense that *Christianity is true religion.* Christianity teaches you a *process* of humility, waiting, ego surrender, patience and trust, much more than merely giving you prefabricated *content* to defend or prove. Some Hindus and Buddhists have this true religion much more than many Christians. Many of us prefer only ways of thinking over a process of transformation, which always asks us to "die."

Erasmus the Reconstructionist

At the very end of the medieval era, as the Reformation was challenging all of the old paradigms with new ways of thinking and relating, Erasmus of Rotterdam (1466-1536) charted a course of reconstruction. Perhaps you've heard of him. There probably would have been no painful dividing of Europe over the Reformation if Erasmus had been listened to instead of the pope on one side and Luther on the other. Dualistic thinking won and therefore we all lost. Either/or thinking never leaves room for the wonderful "third something." Erasmus was a third-something person.

Erasmus stood patiently in the middle and said that there was truth in both what the pope and in what Luther was saying. (Only four hundred and fifty years later, in 1999, did the Catholics and Lutherans agree that they had been saying the same thing!) But Erasmus, by and large, was unheeded. He calmly kept speaking, trying to persuade each to see the other's side, but both were trapped in their own ideological hysteria—the same pattern we see in so many places and groups today. The divided mind led to a divided and warring Europe, and Christian divisions that last to this day.

Erasmus stressed actions over formal theology: He held that there should be an absolute minimum of theology. In that we see a similarity with the reconstructive approach of Saint Francis. True spirituality doesn't require much middle management. You just basically have to teach people how to see and then they'll see for themselves. Of course, teaching people how to see isn't easy, because you also have to teach them to see *all the way through and to see everything*. It's major surgery to get that ego and those private agendas out of the way so you can see. Erasmus emphasized epistemology over metaphysics, *how* you see over *what* you see.

The best ally of God is reality—not theology, not ideology, not what *should be* as much as what *is*. Erasmus said, "No Christian—especially no child—needs or is capable of digesting the thoroughgoing encyclopedic catechism that gives an answer for every conceivable question that we could possibly run into—and the answer in fact makes the journey unnecessary."

Erasmus felt it was precisely that mindset that had gotten the Church in trouble for much of its fifteen hundred-year history, and then Luther too, thinking the catechism could and should explain everything. Erasmus questioned, "Is it not possible to have a fellowship with the Father, Son and Holy Spirit without being able to explain philosophically the distinction between them?" He was saying then what liberation theologians are saying now, that Jesus clearly taught orthopraxy (right behavior) much more than orthodoxy (right ideas).

I think the Church is going to have to come to respect the limits of human understanding and the limits of its own understanding of mystery. Strangely, it teaches the first but denies the second. The institutional Church has to get beyond needing answers and theological conclusions for every possible scenario that arises. And yet we are the very ones who love to preserve the notion of mystery! I do not think you can have it both ways. We should be the protectors of mystery, not the explainers of it. Probably it's a natural outgrowth of the Greco-Roman model of organization that influenced us so much. The Eastern Church seems much more comfortable with mystery.

Cynics are often those who once expected too much. But when you put all your eggs in one basket—expecting everything from this institution—you're setting yourself up for major disappointment. I think that's behind a lot of the disillusionment that so many Catholics have gone through in recent years. Yes, we need to take the institution seriously, just about as seriously as Jesus took the institution of Judaism. My point is that we shouldn't take it overly seriously. Jesus critiqued Judaism radically. As in the rest of life, we need to say yes to something before we're free to say no. But we must also say no when needed, or we have idolatry, the major sin of the Hebrew Scriptures.

The Case of the Birth Control Encyclical

Let me give you a difficult, unpopular example. One of the encyclicals (papal teachings) that has probably been most criticized is Pope Paul VI's 1968 encyclical, *Humanae Vitae* (*On Human Life*). The media, and most of the Church, picked up on its prohibition of artificial birth control and missed all the rest. Many of its critics haven't read it. *Humanae Vitae*'s theology is excellent, but liberals assume it has nothing to say, and conservatives bow down in front of it before they have read it. This is not the wonderful third something, but leaves us both in our split minds.

In fact, most of the sense of limits, goals and values in the encyclical are really excellent. And I would bet that ninety-five percent of the read-ers of this book would say the same thing if we actually read it. But we seem never to get beyond either a Western mistrust of authority or an ideological bias toward all authority. Authority and truth are really not the same principle. *Jesus came to give us a truth that would set us free, not an authority that would do all our homework for us.* Institutional religion is doing God no favor by setting up a professional teaching station, which itself becomes the issue instead of the gospel values themselves. We either love this teaching station or we hate it, and never get to "justice, mercy, and good faith" (Matthew 22:23).

Instead of a thinking and faithful people, we live, like our culture as a whole, with sound bites and one-liners. We react against the whole thing uncritically or buy the whole thing uncritically—instead of saying, "What are the values here that are worth listening to? What are the truths here about marital love, faithful love, about communication and relationship?" That's the big point of *Humanae Vitae*, by the way: communication between husband and wife, mutual respect, mutuality. This is the same agenda that the feminists are rightly seeking.

For us as Christians, the highest value is always love. If you're going to accept the Judeo-Christian heritage as meaningful and authoritative in any way, you have to admit that love comes first and last. That puts you on a different track and forces a different set of questions. The deepest questions are not those of rights and power, and whether or not I'm getting everything that society owes me. The deepest questions are those of how can love be expanded and increased. How can we "defer to one another out of reverence for Christ" (Ephesians 5:21)?

This is a third way, a "new something" wonderful. The dualistic and merely political mind will never understand it. It reads everything in terms of win/lose, right/wrong, good/bad, either/or, top/bottom. Only the contemplative mind, the new consciousness made possible by God-experience and prayer, can read reality in a panoramic and truly wisdom fashion (see 1 Corinthians 2:12-16 in this regard). The calculating mind, the egocentric vision, is all that the system has. We have a new mind made possible by God.

CHAPTER TWELVE

Living With Darkness

· · · · · · · · · · · · · ·

SPIRITUAL TRANSFORMATION is often thought of as movement from darkness to light. In one sense that is true, but in another sense it is totally false. We forget that darkness is always present alongside the light. Pure light blinds, only the mixture of darkness and light allows us to see. Shadows are required for our seeing. God alone lives in perfect light (James 1:17).

In a certain sense, you could say that we know the light most fully in contrast with its opposite—the dark. Christian theology has traditionally talked about the "happy fault," the idea that if Christ had not been crucified, he would not have experienced the Resurrection. Again we see that there is something you can only know by going through "the night sea journey" into the belly of the whale, from which you are spit up on an utterly new shore.

Western civilization has failed to learn how to carry the dark side. We did not evangelize through our living icon, Jesus. Instead, we brought a system involving winners and losers, which is not Jesus. Now because we did not teach our people how to carry the paschal mystery, it is coming back to haunt us. Catholics have no ability to carry the dark side of the Church either, nor the dark side of the papacy, nor the dark side of the clergy. It is always all good or all bad, never "both crucified and resurrected at the same time," as Jesus is. Catholic politics is not known worldwide for creating negotiators, mediators, compromise or peacemaking. Let's be humble enough to admit it, and weep over our sins. In that sense, we are not the hope of the world!

In many ways it's been a constant dilemma of the Church. It wants to live in perfect light, where God alone lives. It does not like the shadowland called earth, its only home. We see in Christian history the Eastern Church trying to create heavenly liturgies with little sense of social justice, Luther's abhorrence of his own darkness; the Swiss Reformers trying to outlaw darkness; the Puritans trying to repress darkness; the Roman Church consistently unable and unwilling to see its own darkness; the typical believer afraid of darkness, the new fundamentalists splitting darkness off into a preoccupation with Satan. Then comes the postmodern world, in predictable pendulum swing, in love with darkness! All of us, it seems, are trying to find ways to avoid the human mystery, instead of learning how to carry it patiently, as our humble Jesus did.

There are no perfect structures and there are no perfect people. There is only the struggle to get there. It is Christ's passion (*patior*, the "suffering of reality") that will save the world. "Your patient endurance will win you your lives," says Luke (21:19). Redemptive suffering instead of redemptive violence is the Jesus way. Patience comes from our attempts to hold together an always-mixed reality, not from expecting or demanding a perfect reality. That only makes us resentful and judgmental, which is what has characterized much of Christian history. I agree with Bishop Spong when he says, "I don't like religious people very much." Who likes people who can never deal patiently with darkness and shadow, which is just about everything?

Nietzsche said that one reason he could not trust Christians is because they seemed to be so filled with "resentment." False expectations create resentful people, like Sisyphus rolling the stone up the hill, knowing it will roll back down. Grateful people emerge in a world rightly defined, where even the darkness is no surprise, but is in fact opportunity.

Our failure to carry the darkness as individuals has moved to a secular level, too. We refuse to carry the dark side of institutions, of groups, nations, of periods of history. We look for races and nations to blame, instead of admitting that we are all in this human thing together. Every culture, in my opinion, is a mixture of darkness and light.

There is not much point in deciding the exact percentages, or, like children, fighting over who hit whom first. Go back far enough, and we all oppressed others or were oppressed ourselves. There is no moral high ground on which to stand in the big picture. Whoever has the power, oppresses. You can take that as normative, and it includes native peoples, Jews, blacks and women. When they are on top they do the same thing. Jesus reframed the question around power, not ethnicity, religion or gender. He stepped out of the whole cycle by riding into the human city "on a donkey," outside the symbols of power. Maybe we avoid darkness because it is an in-depth experience of our own powerlessness and poverty.

None of us want to be a part of any imperfect group or institution. Perhaps because we did not resolve the question on a personal level, we have no ability to deal with it on a historical level. We keep looking for some perfect pedestal to stand on, some place where we can be clean and pure and above it all. Remember, the very notion of religion begins with the creating of the concept of impurity. Jesus ended religion, as we know it, forever.

Learning in Darkness

Darkness is a good and a necessary teacher. It is not to be avoided, denied, run from or explained away. It's not even too quickly to be forgiven. First, like Ezekiel the Prophet, we must eat the scroll that is "lamentation, wailing, and moaning" in our belly, and only eventually sweet as honey (see Ezekiel 3:1-3). When we're in darkness, there's a loss of meaning and motivation. By the time most people reach middle age they have experienced days when they just can't find life—joy isn't there. We call it depression, and some form of it happens to most people at some time. In its extreme form, it requires medical attention. But clinical depression is not what we're talking about here (although it could take that form if we do not find God in it).

There's a darkness that we are led into by our own stupidity, by our own sin, by our own selfishness, by living out of the false self. We have to work our way back out of these by brutal honesty, confessions and surrenders, some forgiveness, and often by some necessary restitution or apology. The old language would have called it repentance, penance or stripping. By any account, it is major surgery and feels like dying (although it also feels like immense liberation). We need help at these times. Alcoholics Anonymous seems to be very good in its advice at this stage, even for non-alcoholics.

There's another darkness, however, that we're led into by God and grace, and the nature of the journey itself. In many ways the loss of meaning here is even greater. And sometimes the loss of motivation is greater. The loss of purpose, boundaries, directions might be greater, too. It really feels like darkness, and thus the saints called it "the dark night." But the difference is that we still sense that we have been led here intentionally somehow. We know we are in "liminal space," betwixt and between, on the threshold—and we have to stay there until we have learned something essential. It is still no fun, and filled with doubt and "demons" of every sort. But it is the darkness of God. All transformation takes place in such liminal space.

Now the darknesses that we lead ourselves into by sin can also become the darkness of God. Maybe it is even the most common pattern. But there is nevertheless a "good darkness" and a "bad darkness," basically having to do with whether we see God in it. The wound can become the sacred wound, or it can just remain a bleeding useless wound with a scab that never heals. *Salvation is most commonly sin overcome in the biblical tradition, not just sin avoided.* It's the sin that becomes salvation. But it's the same event, the same experience.

In times of darkness there's usually an overwhelming sense of not belonging, of not fitting in. Have you had those days when you feel nothing will console you, and the old things that you used to do no longer work? There's no friend to call today who could take this pain away. That's when, of course, we're driven to prayer. We either find God then, or go into a deep freeze.

Normally there's a reluctance to talk to helpful people, or to the people we once trusted. This feels like an act of rebellion against any kind of help. We close down. Many of my generation said proudly, "Don't trust anybody over thirty!" We had seen our father figures almost totally sell out to militarism and materialism. We could not trust them as mentors of spirituality or wisdom. We hated their darkness and then fell into our own. Unfortunately, we seem now to be experiencing a universal non-trust, a universal rebellion. Why should I trust any politician or priest or president? They've shown that they are not good leaders. We are, of course, half right. But there is another half.

We're often rebelling against our own inner priesthood, our own inner prophet who might know the way for us. We're almost choosing to sit in the darkness. And maybe that has to be, too. Normally, in the darkness, there's restlessness, a type of inner pacing. It's almost as if the going backward and forward on the same path is an image of who you are, not really wanting to go any direction, just turning around as if you're going to find the answer in between. Maybe we need this deconstruction before we can rightly reconstruct on the foundations of the True Self.

In that restlessness, you not only can't pray, you don't want to pray. Of course, then you are throwing out the only inner authority you might have, or the only wisdom you might trust. You don't even want to trust God. You don't want to do so because God might have an answer, and then you would have to act. You don't want to act. The tragic, the paralysis, the self-pity have a strange attraction.

When we have reached this point, we usually start looking for someone to blame. The stupidity of blaming is that it absolves us from solving the problem within ourselves. Blaming will not do the soul work, it will not remain with the paradox. It splits instead, and releases the *eustress* (good stress), the creative anxiety. Yet staying with the paradox, the *eustress*, refusing to compartmentalize the good and the bad, might be the most courageous thing we have ever done.

To stay with the paradox is an immense act of courage, and why some moralists have said courage is the foundational virtue. The word courage comes from *cor-agere*, "an act of the heart," which we now know has its own kind of intelligence (see *The HeartMath Solution*, by Doc Childre and Howard Martin, with Donna Beech, HarperSanFrancisco, 1999). Now we know that all our poetry and music about "the heart" was not just poetry and music but correct intuition.

While experiencing a sense of loss of meaning it is very difficult to try to self-generate courage; you can only draw it from others. You look for signs around you that maybe life has meaning for someone else. You wait for positive contagion. Sometimes you just look for a smile. I've experienced that in little ways from simple kindnesses of store clerks, or from small exchanges at the kiss of peace during Mass. I may have been just going through the motions of Mass, and then at the kiss of peace some loving, good person looks into my eyes and really seems to mean it and say it, and I come back to the altar transformed. What it comes down to so often is the power of simple love to lead us out of meaninglessness. It sounds so naive and so simplistic, but love is still the greatest healer, the great transformer and the greatest giver of meaning. Love aligns you. Yet during times of darkness, love is the very thing we resist and almost make impossible. "I will prove that I am unworthy. I will not let you get to me." There is an almost demonic energy at that point. That is the real darkness of the dark periods. There is no way out from within.

Good Doubt

In darkness we doubt everything. For most people, deep change starts with doubt about day-to-day things. Then they move into mental doubts, then ethical doubt about who is right and who is wrong and finally they move into absolute doubt or total cynicism. To change fundamentally you have to go all the way to the bottom. And when you're at the point of absolute doubt then you, hopefully, look for new meanings (although some people remain there and make skepticism a way of life). There are many signs that some aspects of our culture today are fixed in a state of absolute doubt. It is only good to pass through there, but not to stay there.

Out of the chaos often comes the greatest creativity. And the only thing that can endure deep doubt is faith. You will not allow yourselves to go into the deeper levels of doubting without, in fact, a very strong faith. That's just the opposite of what most people think. I fault the tradition here for telling us that doubt was a bad thing. Those who can endure great doubt, in my experience, have been those who rise to great faith. Faith gets purified every time you go through the cycle of doubt and failure, saying, "Why do I believe this? Do I believe this at all? What do I base my life on?" On this wheel of fortune just about everything is purified: self-image, God-image, worldview.

If there was compassion and forgiveness in someone's first models of authority, then there is undoubtedly a readiness to believe a God of compassion and forgiveness. So, of course, people who have been surrounded by compassion and love have a great big head-start on the true image of God and reality in general.

It takes a long time to purify the experience of dysfunctional family life, abuse, manipulation, shaming, negative attitudes toward anything, totalitarian attitudes or judgmental attitudes. They're only purified in desperate and dark situations where the old god doesn't work any more, the old self and old attitudes don't work anymore. As Saint John of the Cross described, our gods must each die till we find the true God. Or as Meister Eckhart put it, "I pray to God to rid me of God." But each dying god is another darkness and another death, which is probably why the great mystics speak of darkness so much.

Cultural Darkness and Crisis

I think we've been led into a period of exile again, both as a culture and as a Church. In the periods of darkness we feel a lot of hostility. We take it out on other people by blaming them. But often all it takes to stem this is for one person to take a hopeful stance. I remember one time I was sitting with a family who had just come back from Sunday morning Mass. They were pretty much damning the morning Mass and the priest—I guess it wasn't a very good liturgy or homily. The father of the family calmly brought another perspective. He said, "Listen, I have my bad days. Can't we give him credit, he had a bad day today." Suddenly the whole tone changed, by the quiet leadership of a father of a family. Imagine how dead-ended and useless it would have been if he simply joined in on the lynching. I am not saying there is no place for criticism, but there is the kind that opens possibility and the kind that merely spews and increases negative energy.

There's a lot of freedom in being able to say something like he did in a crowd going in the opposite direction. It takes spaciousness inside of you to give spaciousness to others. In this case he gave space for both the priest and for his family to grow. Maybe spaciousness is a good definition of compassion. It is certainly a good description of a third way.

The temptation in times of darkness is to pull back from others, to move into a self-chosen exile. Then evil festers, because evil festers when people are cut off, which happens to be my criticism of so much of the prison system. Whenever you separate people in a state of alienation, evil festers; it doesn't decrease. It's the same when we pull into our personal prisons, our chosen exiles. That's when marriages end, when there's a refusal to remain in the dialogue. The very word *diabolical* means to "throw apart." Thus, the insidious nature of modern individualism: We cannot retreat there, although it is a great temptation in confused times, such as now.

Much pulling back is not out of discernment so that I can hear better, like the desert retreats of Jesus. But a lot of pulling back is more often out of fear, and sometimes out of contempt for others, or perhaps for the Church because it has not served us well. I wonder if some people's rejections are not an extended form of their own self-loathing. No one is more anti-Catholic than Catholics, it seems. No one bemoans, betrays and tears down their own tradition more than Christians. People who hate themselves hate others just like them.

When spiritual issues are not resolved in our own lives, when compassion is not found in our immediate sphere, we hate the groups and the history and the ancestry we're a part of. We overreact against it. Here again is the refusal to carry the dark side, this time the dark side of my own tradition. And those of us who are Catholic have a long tradition to carry, two thousand years of silliness—and two thousand years of saints.

We are formed both by "the right hand of God" and "the left hand of God." The right hand of God is always the gratuity, the wonder, the "ah, the loveliness of life." But the left hand of God is always the painful mystery of things. And the left hand of God is just as essential in our formation as the right hand of God. It is the whomp on the side of the head that gets our necessary attention. Then we can hear and receive and need something new and good.

The way through is always much more difficult than the way around. Cheap religion gives us the way around. True religion gives us the way through. Cheap religion denies the darkness. True religion steps right into it.

The Traps Inside

When you're in the shame-and-blame game, which is where we are when we're in darkness, you'll usually be a master of projection. We know that our hatred of others is normally a projection of our own inner state. That's why Jesus taught that, for the sake of *your* soul, you *must* love the enemy. The enemy carries your dark side. Look carefully for those you resent, because they're normally carrying at least some of what you hate or deny or reject within yourself. Again, Jesus said it first: "Why do you try to take the speck out of your brother or sister's eye, when you cannot see the log in your own?" (Matthew 7:5). Normally, it is here before it is there.

We allow our feelings out against the group or against the community, instead of realizing that this is a time when the Lord can teach us. "Perhaps this is a lesson. How can I learn from this too?," we must say. Normally, at that point we do need a spiritual friend; it's almost impossible to pull yourself out of the pit alone. Someone else has to "preach the gospel" to us. I know, as a preacher, that I usually cannot preach to myself.

We also need a guide because we're in uncharted territory. We don't know how to get out of the darkness, so it's easier to just sit there and justify being there. We tend to seek out friends who give us the justification for being there, who keep bemoaning the terrible situation and legitimate our hurts. It's Job sitting on the dung heap, and his stupid friends giving him further reasons for staying there. Remember how he picked at his sores with a potsherd (Job 2:8). We keep replaying the old tapes and re-biting ("re-morse") the old sour food. Just like Job, we sit on our dung heap for seven days and seven nights (2:13).

The temptation of your group, your family, your community is to be threatened by your negativity. They don't want to hear it, perhaps because they might be drawn in by the truth that's there. Some fear all critical thinking because they fear that the structures will collapse. You see this in so many of the neoconservatives who cannot tolerate any criticism of the Church, or the patriots and flag-worshipers of America.

There is such a thing as healthy criticism. People who love something have also earned the right to make it better and keep it true to its deepest vision. All criticism is not blind negativity; it can also carry hope and vision when you own the problem. When you recognize that you are an accomplice in the evil and also complicit in the good, and take responsibility for both, when you can use the language of "we" and not "them," then you are bearing the full mystery of something. Your criticism is coming from love, not hate.

Two Sides of Truth

In general the only people I really trust doing reconstruction work are people who have paid their dues to deconstruction. If someone has never been able to see the dark side, they haven't gained the right to talk the language of reconstruction. You need to have seen the dark side, have felt the sour stomach and have emerged renewed from the belly of the whale. We don't need naive people or people in denial. We need people who have been there, know the problems and have come out alive.

You need to have pulled away from the idolatry of the system in order to gain the authority and the credibility to walk back in and to work for reconstruction.

If all you can do is criticize and negatively point out the dark side, however, you have another set of problems. There's no gift of hope or positive energy here; there is only paralysis. An insecure community or group cannot tolerate criticism. As I said earlier in this book, it was a sign of the maturity of the Church that it could self-criticize during the Second Vatican Council in the 1960's. A healthy family can—in fact, must—own its dirty laundry. As the alcoholics say, "we are as sick as our secrets." And we are as healthy as the way we criticize.

Whatever you say about the 1960's that began the current deconstruction in earnest, it was a healthy period of self-criticism of culture and Church. How different from the idolatry of the 1980's when both pope and president (Reagan) could no longer allow criticism! America was the promised land and the Catholic Church was the only way to go to heaven again. It is especially strange that the Church, which insists, "sins cannot be forgiven without naming them in confession according to kind, number, and intention," has been unable to do the same. Thank God, Pope John Paul II began to correct this long pattern of corporate pride and nonrepentance in his public confessions of Lent 2000.

Darkness is sacred ground. Our trust is that the God who has called us into this present darkness will also sustain us and lead us through it. Undoubtedly we're in a period of potentially transformative darkness. In a certain sense there is only one definition of the biblical God. Yahweh and his servant Jesus are always the ones "who bring the dead to life and call into being what does not yet exist" (see both Deuteronomy 32:39 and Romans 4:17). It is the one and only pattern of God, and we are ready for it again and always.

While material goods decrease as we make use of them, spiritual goods increase as we use them. We are ready to make use of our immense spiritual power. What is genuinely exciting is that many of these gospel gifts are being discovered and used outside the explicit community of faith, since we seem to have neglected them. I don't suppose God cares which group gets the credit. It is all God's work anyway, and when *A Course in Miracles* (a self-study course in spiritual psychology), Alcoholics Anonymous, along with prison reform systems, social workers and ecologists make use of spiritual power, it will only increase and spread. Maybe Jesus was speaking of his own community when he warned against burying the gift out of fear (see Luke 19:20) instead of using it with abandon.

The religious worldview is essentially hope-filled. Any experience of grace tells us that history is not about us. In fact, my own life is not about me! History is more than human history; it's also God's history, the planet's history, the history of the life and death of God in all things. Who would not want to be a part of that? Sometimes I find archeologists, nurses, marine biologists and Hindu mothers of six who enter trustfully into this great mystery more than those of us who have been officially baptized into it. They are useable for God.

Toppling the Idols

As we get closer to the real thing, the opposition will rise, just as it rose around Jesus. It's very scary whenever you're moving to a new synthesis or paradigm, especially to those who are heavily invested in the old. They usually have much to lose. They are not necessarily of ill will; it's just that they're living in the only world they've ever imagined.

Human beings tend to live inside of their small comfort zones. We put all of our trust and security in institutions, in jobs, in explanations, even in sacred things like family. It's no surprise that Jesus has to call the first disciples away not from "bad" things, but good things like family and job (see Mark 1:19-20).

The role of the prophet is to direct and legitimate necessary deconstruction, the deconstructing of what I would call the false self. His is the path of the descent, and is never popular nor easy. It is about letting go of illusion and toppling of false gods. The prophets are always killed.

People will feel you are being negative or violent when you deconstruct their false worlds, because that is all they have. If you've built your whole life around your job and your reputation, you naturally don't want to let go of them. You will fight not to die. Ultimately, however, the naming and dismantling of the false self is profoundly liberating. But we have yet to learn that.

In spirituality, there are basically two paths: the path of the fall and the path of the return. The path of the fall is directed and legitimated by the prophets who teach us how to go into darkness creatively, how to let things fall apart. They teach us how to lose gracefully, how to let go without fear. They are God's deconstructionists.

The other path is the path of the return. That's been the role of the priestly class. True priests talk of union, communion, love, transcendence, religion, connecting this world and the next world and giving back a coherent world of meaning. Everybody usually likes the priests and they quickly become establishment and comfortable in almost all cultures.

We've had way too much priesthood and not nearly enough prophesy, in my humble opinion. The result often has been religion for religion's sake, all path of the return with no path of the fall. How can you return to a new world when you have never fallen away from the old one? Priests tell self-satisfied people about communion with God, yet their God and their need is still so small, or even false. How can you know the light if you've never named the darkness?

CHAPTER THIRTEEN

Modern Models of Reconstruction

· ·

I'D LIKE TO CLOSE this book with a look at a few people who, as twentieth- (and twenty-first-) century Americans, have helped to put together the reconstruction theme in a practical, yet non-ideological way. What you find in Dorothy Day, for example, you find in most prophetic types: an almost simplistic traditionalism. She didn't have time to challenge the traditions of Church while she was pouring all her energy into changing society, too. That makes sense: I'm told that you cannot be fully committed to a group and be radically trying to change it at the same time. Theoretically, yes, but practically it seldom works out that way. The ground beneath your feet must be solid and not filled with suspicion itself.

I've seen this clear pattern in my own experience of community, in my experience of lay communities and in my Franciscan community, too. Someone would reach a point of serious doubt and decide to campaign to change the group at its core. It was just a matter of months before they'd leave. To critique a group you have to be committed to it in an essential and ongoing way. *You have to have said a deep yes before you can dare to say no or you die inside the group.* Thus, the only people who can effectively criticize anything are those who have made the surrender first—the believers. Too often, I find the critics among those who have "paid no dues" to the upbuilding of the group, almost as if their criticism is an excuse not to commit "until it is like I want it." That doesn't work! True prophets are *always* from within the group, never throwing stones from outside where they have no responsibility for picking up the pieces.

Believers can afford to be critics. But what we have in modern nihilism are critics who believe in nothing. They've made no surrenders, but take pot shots living around the edge of everything. They're accountable to no group or institution. They're accountable to no personal God, but always waiting to place their bets. In many ways, it is a lack of courage, the quality which, as we said, might be the primary virtue. It is the refusal to take the great leap of faith.

So here are a few contemporary examples of people who point toward the kind of loving rebuilding that we are calling reconstruction. This list is just a small sample, but these people offer inspiration to those who would build a culture of meaning, one anchored in tradition, yet open to the future, formed by what I called before "transformative traditionalism." After their stories, I'll end with a creed for rebuilders, which will hopefully inspire you as you go forth and rebuild.

Dorothy Day

Dorothy Day is well known as the founder of the Catholic Worker Movement in New York. She was a journalist who took Church teaching about solidarity with the poor at face value. Whether on the picket lines or in soup kitchens, she always remained faithful and close to the people she felt called by the gospel to serve, but she always remained a faithful believer inside the Church "container" too. For her, faith lived in the Church was the foundation of her radical commitment to social change.

Dorothy paid her dues and I want to quote her: "I love the Church for Christ-made vision, not for itself. Because it's usually a scandal to me." Now there's a great and terrible lover. Early in the twentieth century, Romano Guardini said almost the same thing, cited earlier in this book: "The Church is the cross on which Christ is always crucified. One cannot separate Christ from His cross. And one cannot separate Christ from His bloody painful Church. One must live in a state of permanent dissatisfaction with the Church." Wow! This was an orthodox Italian monsignor speaking.

Cardinal Joseph Bernardin

I had the privilege of knowing Chicago's Cardinal Bernardin when he was archbishop of Cincinnati and I was leading the New Jerusalem community. He was a holy man already then, and he continued through his life with an ever-deeper commitment to building bridges across chasms. He worked tirelessly to heal the breech between Jews and Christians, conservatives and liberals, rich and poor, militarists and pacifists, and to build unity within the Christian family wherever he was.

When he died in 1997, Chicago grieved for three full days while his body lay in state in the cathedral. The leaders of most Christian denominations in the region held a memorial service as part of the funeral rituals. For the first time ever, the Jewish community, too, held a memorial service for a cardinal of the Catholic Church, right there in the Catholic cathedral while he lay in state! He represented that larger-than-life mind that is Christ.

He had been falsely accused of a sexual allegation three years earlier and put himself before the media and his fellow bishops openly and without shame, professing the truth. Eventually his accuser admitted the story wasn't true, and Joseph Bernardin flew to Philadelphia to pray with this sick and dying man. How it must have hurt him that some people—even some colleagues—clearly believed the false accusation!

It was no surprise to me that he showed such virtue in his last years because I will always remember the risks that he took for me and the friendship that he showed me over many years. I was a young upstart, clearly able to embarrass him, yet he always treated me like a son. He never rebuked me, but would simply talk with me about the many complaints against me, the transcribed accounts of "heretical" teaching, the occasional breaking of Church rules and liturgical rules for what I thought were gospel values. He would never forbid me or threaten me, like other bishops later did, but he would simply say, "If you feel called to do this again, let's talk about it beforehand," or in relation to my spontaneous style of liturgy, he once said, "I know you have a good sense of what prayerful liturgy should be. I trust you, but just don't videotape your Mass." He did not give me license, but instead a desire to grow and be responsible.

Then Joseph Bernardin himself fell ill with cancer at an early age. Yet he learned to call this darkness of death his "friend." He dropped all administrative duties and began visiting the sick himself because now he understood. Month after month he stood in front of the TV cameras and let the world watch him weaken and yet remain faithful. He said his ministry was merely an imitation of the Good Shepherd, seeking out the lost sheep, as opposed to merely keeping the other sheep penned in.

He told me once privately that the impromptu metaphor about "the seamless garment theology" would probably be the only thing he would be remembered for. Yet over the three days of memorial services, people stood in a line sometimes five blocks long to pay their respect to him and what he stood for. We obviously remember him for much more as well. He continued to work positively to create, and more to live "a consistent ethic of life."

Vjeko Curic, O.F.M.

In the bloodbath that was Rwanda in the 1990's, this Franciscan friar became a martyr for peace. Curic himself was a Croatian whose own country was being torn into pieces by the disintegration of Yugoslavia and the inter-ethnic warfare and genocide that took place between Catholic Croats, Muslims and Orthodox Serbs.

Much of the same ethnic hatred fueled what happened in the missionary region of Rwanda where he worked in parish ministry from 1983 until his 1997 death. As the racial conflict heightened between the tribal Hutus and Tutsis, Western Church workers began packing their bags. But Curic insisted upon remaining behind, pleading for people to find peaceful means to resolve their deep differences. He selflessly worked to help the victims of both nations. He also brought numerous whites (bishops, priests, monks, nuns and others) to safety. Curic reminds us of Jesus crucified, holding his arms out in both directions, embracing the opposites and bringing them together.

On January 31, 1997, outside his parish home in Kigali, assassins came and shot him to death. Deconstruction cannot live in the presence of reconstructionists.

Paula Gonzalez, S.C.

She's a woman on a mission to save the earth—literally. Sister Paula, a Ph.D. biologist and Catholic sister, turned in her mature years toward becoming a full-time recycler and ecological educator. She travels throughout the United States, imploring people to take ecology seriously—she sees Western culture on a ruinous path of ecological disaster. And she knows that care of creation is a human activity that happens one person at a time.

For years she was a voice crying in the wilderness. (Reconstructionists often are.) Yet she persisted, finding something as simple as her annual yard sale (she's sold $160,000 worth of "junk" over twenty years!) as a way to teach people to stop throwing things away. For her birthday each year people bring all manner of recycled goods as presents, much to her delight!

On an abandoned farm owned by her religious community she organized a group of volunteers to convert a chicken coop into a passive solar apartment, using mostly recycled materials. She and another sister have lived there ever since.

Years later she founded EarthConnection, an environmental education program that teaches participants how to understand the effects of industrial society and how to take practical steps to re-integrate with creation.

She is deeply tied to nature, growing a large garden each year in the tradition of her New Mexican family of origin. A native of the "Land of Enchantment," she literally loves the sun. Not only does she find in the sun the best way to heat her home, but, like Saint Francis, she draws her life energy from creation. Nature regenerates and rebuilds itself constantly. It is that reconstructive energy that Gonzalez brings to the human family. In the words of her father, who taught her to garden, "*La tierra es bendita*" — "the earth is sacred."

We are very blessed that the guest house for the Center for Action and Contemplation in the South Valley of Albuquerque, Tepeyac, was originally the Gonzales family home. The central part is true handmade adobe, and it was there that Paula first connected with many of these earth issues. We are hoping that we are carrying on her work and vision at Tepeyac, which is now a center for Permaculture, simple living experiments, and oft-times temporary housing for refugee families and homeless folks. There really is an "energy" to places and lands. Of all the houses in Albuquerque, how did we end up with her house! We hope we are continuing her wonderful reconstruction, even with only half of her energy.

Tom and Molly Carew

Tom Carew and Molly Barrett first came to work in the Appalachian mountains of eastern Kentucky in the early 1970's as student volunteers — Tom from Queens, New York; Molly from St. Paul, Minnesota. Soon they discovered each other and a common vision of faith, hope, love — and seemingly boundless energy. They married and sunk roots in Morehead, Kentucky. Tom had already founded Frontier Housing, a nonprofit company that since 1974 has built over four hundred houses and renovated two hundred others in an area where warm, dry housing simply wasn't an option for thousands of people. Molly, a nurse by training, has conducted a ministry of home-health medicine over the years, though she focused her energy on maintaining her own home from the time their first child was born until their fourth and youngest was in school. Now she is a nurse-practitioner, providing medical care in a rural county that would have none without her small clinic.

Molly and Tom show the way for those who would be married, raise children and yet remain committed to rebuilding the world around them. We don't find so many famous people in this arena; indeed our culture and Church have been unable somehow to put forward the normal, married lifestyle as a place from which society is rebuilt. Yet the home, what we used to call the Domestic Church, is the place where reconstructive energy is woven into children's very psyche (see Chapter Three on family rituals for more on this).

Just as Tom has literally rebuilt houses for families, Molly has helped to bring the medical care that rebuilds lives and families. In the midst of this reconstructive energy, both have encountered difficult personal and family choices. For Tom it was the opportunity to be national director of Habitat for Humanity. He turned down the offer because he and Molly felt it would not be good for their children to move at that time. For Molly, it was the resounding yes to mother her children that meant no to professional opportunities. They both say, in retrospect, that their choices, though painful, were the right, most life-giving choices.

Along the way, the Carews always found time to build community with those outside their family, picking up one of the beautiful themes of Appalachian culture. Weddings of friends became pot-luck events; always there was time for a talk on the porch swing, a drive across several counties for a weekend visit or just a simple, caring act of charity for a family in need.

A Reconstructionist Creed

. . . .

NOW, THEN, LET US END on a hopeful note. Let us, as Saint Francis said, begin again. Allow the following creed to inspire your efforts to rebuild.

> We believe in one God. "There is one Body, one Spirit, one and the same hope. . . one Lord, one faith, one baptism, one God who is Father of all, over all, through all, and within all" (Ephesians 4:4-6).

> We believe that we are, first of all, a people, God's movement in history.

> We believe that our individual lives and our personal growth are for the sake of the generation to come after and built on the faith and the bones of those who have gone ahead of us.

> We believe that we must build on the positive, on what you love. Creative and life energies come from belief and from commitment. Critics must first be believers who have learned how to say an ultimate yes.

> We agree to bear the burden and the grace of our past. We agree to honor what is, which includes even the broken things of life: ourselves, Church, state and all institutions. The dark side of each of these is a good and necessary teacher.

> We are committed to building a world of meaning and hope. We recognize the clear need for prophetic deconstruction of all idolatries that make the worship of God impossible. True rebuilding must follow this temporary but necessary unbuilding.

> We believe in a personal universe where the divine image shines through all created things. It is therefore an "enchanted

universe" where we can always live in reverence and even adoration before the good, the true and the beautiful.

Along with Saint Paul in Colossians (1:15-20), as Christians, we believe that Jesus is the clearest image of the unseen God. In him all things cohere, all opposites are overcome. He is the head of the living body in whom all things are reconciled and overcome.

Epilogue

· · · · · ·

'You see the trouble we are in: Jerusalem is in ruins.... *Come, let us rebuild the walls of Jerusalem and suffer this indignity no longer...Let us start! ...Let us build';* and with willing hands they set about the good work. *(The Book of Nehemiah 2:17-18)*

Brothers, let us begin again, for up to now we have done nothing. *(Saint Francis of Assisi near his death)*